SOUTH BANK

ARCHITECTURE & DESIGN

SOUTH BANK

DOMINIC BRADBURY
PHOTOGRAPHED BY RACHAEL SMITH

ARCHITECTURE
& DESIGN

BATSFORD

CONTENTS

INTRODUCTION

London's South Bank has a unique character all of its own. The setting, on the edge of the capital's great winding waterway, encapsulates a powerful sense of national optimism, yet also serves as a focal point – in many respects – for creative experimentation, embracing the arts, architecture and the wider cultural life of the country. The South Bank plays host to a collection of our most important and influential post-war institutions, including the Royal Festival Hall and the National Theatre, while many of these buildings also provide key landmarks in the evolution of British architecture.

The riverside here was, famously, the chosen site for the Festival of Britain in 1951. Apart from London's County Hall, which was largely completed by 1922, this stretch of the Thames was still dominated by wharves, factories and power stations during the Forties, when the site was first suggested as a suitable location for the Festival. The clear advantages offered by the South Bank included its proximity to central London and its major transport hubs, as well as offering the open space needed for such an ambitious national event.

The Festival itself marked the 100th anniversary of London's Great Exhibition of 1851 and, like its predecessor, was intended as a celebration of national identity, encompassing a range of carefully curated themes. But, perhaps more importantly, it was widely seen as a moment of renewal or renaissance after the traumas of World War II and continuing austerity, which saw rationing carrying all the way through to 1954. The Festival of Britain was a moment when the country gave thanks but also looked to the future, with technology and modernity providing important strands with the choice of exhibition pavilions.

The vast majority of these pavilions were designed to be temporary, yet there was one key

RIGHT The river and its bridges help to define the South Bank site, with the Royal Festival Hall sitting between the Hungerford and Waterloo Bridges.

exception. The Royal Festival Hall, which also opened in 1951, was not only the major venue and performance space for the Festival itself but was always intended to provide a lynchpin for a new cultural campus situated on the South Bank. The architecture and design of the building offered, arguably, the most complete and rounded expression of the International Style seen in London, and the country more widely, up to that point. It was a symbol of modernism and, in some respects, a statement of intent for the future direction of the South Bank and its architecture.

Yet the subsequent evolution of the former Festival site was, for many reasons, slow and convoluted. Under the guidance of the London County Council's (LCC) architecture department, situated at nearby County Hall, progress was glacial. With the notable exception of the British Film Institute (BFI), which was slotted underneath Waterloo Bridge, very little happened on the site until the early Sixties. By this time, architecture itself had moved on and subsequent buildings such as the Hayward Gallery and Queen Elizabeth Hall adopted a dynamic brutalist style.

Next door, Denys Lasdun was entrusted with the design of the National Theatre at around the same time. Here, again, Lasdun famously embraced concrete and expressed his devotion to layered, stratified structural solutions, creating a building of extraordinary complexity that provides a series of inspiring performance spaces, as well as other communal gathering points, all placed under a single roof. Given the scale and ambition of the National Theatre, it was not completed until 1976 but was also radical in its design philosophy and aesthetic approach. This was a love it or loathe it building, provoking both praise and criticism, becoming one of the most controversial landmarks of the 'style wars', which raged in Britain during the Eighties.

With the opening of the National Theatre, the dream of a cultural campus upon the South Bank was largely realized. The Thames-side site was now home to theatre, art, music and more, with all of these ingredients situated little more than a stone's throw from one another. There

ABOVE & OPPOSITE The South Bank offers both a cultural campus and a waterfront promenade, home to sculptures such as Frank Dobson's *London Pride* (1951).

SOUTHBANK
CENTRE
Roof Garden,
Cafe & Bar

was a catalytic quality to these national institutions, helping to draw incomers such as London Weekend Television (LWT), who built their own headquarters nearby during the Seventies, while just a short walk away IPC Magazines moved into Richard Seifert's King's Reach Tower. Denys Lasdun was also persuaded to return once more to design a new base for IBM, right next door to the National Theatre.

The idea of the South Bank as a microcosm of British architecture continued through the decades, with the journey taking in the International Style, brutalism and important exemplars of adaptive reuse, as seen in the transformation of the OXO Tower from a former factory to a mixed-use building, which included restaurants, galleries, shops and apartments. In the run-up to the millennium, the South Bank was chosen again to serve as a focal point for national celebration and became home to Marks Barfield's Millennium Wheel, better known as the London Eye. Fusing advanced engineering and a fresh architectural approach, the arrival of the great wheel felt very much in keeping with the *avant garde* spirit of the South Bank. Since then, other important attractions have arrived on the South Bank, with the London Aquarium taking up residence in County Hall in 1997, while just along the Thames the Tate Modern opened its doors at the former Bankside Power Station during the year of the millennium.

Since 1951 and the Festival of Britain, the South Bank has become one of London's best loved quarters. The combination of people's palaces, tourist attractions, parks, gardens and a riverside setting – with its many advantages – means that the South Bank has an exceptional position within the cultural life of the capital. It remains as vibrant and engaging as ever.

OPPOSITE The South Bank site provides a microcosm of the evolution of British architecture, including experimental designs and sculptural elements, such as the spiral stairway alongside Queen Elizabeth Hall.

CONTEXT

SITE & SETTING

Today, the South Bank feels very much like an intrinsic part of central London. It is just a short walk from the Strand, over Waterloo Bridge, and has an easy sense of connection with many of the neighbouring quarters, including Covent Garden to the north as well as Southwark and Bankside further along the southern shore of the Thames. It is also well connected to a handful of key transport links, including the river clippers that constantly make their way up and down the river, with the eastern stops reaching as far as Canary Wharf and Greenwich.

It is the Thames itself, of course, which helps to make the South Bank so special. The generous scale of the riverside promenade here ensures enjoyment of the open vistas across the water towards the cityscape beyond, while the river frontage forms an urban parkland in itself, full of light, where the pedestrian takes priority while cars and buses are pushed to the periphery. All of this helps to lend the South Bank a welcoming character all of its own, with the landscaping of both the Queen's Walk promenade and Jubilee Gardens enhancing appreciation of an extraordinary collection of cultural institutions and landmark attractions spread out along the riverside. There is still a sense here, as originally intended back in the Forties and Fifties, of a communal cultural campus that belongs to everyone rather than just a small elite.

ABOVE Beyond Waterloo Bridge sits the National Theatre and a collection of towers, including Richard Seifert's King's Reach, SimpsonHaugh's One Blackfriars and - over to the right - Renzo Piano's Shard.

In many respects, the gift of the riverside setting, combined with its central geographical position within the capital, helped to ensure the success of both the South Bank in general and the 1951 Festival of Britain in particular, which saw millions of visitors arrive here, mostly by public transport, and enjoy what was billed as 'a tonic to the nation'.[1] The restaurants and pavilions created for the Festival were decidedly new and modern, yet the outlook encompassed London's historic cityscape and framed views of the capital's familiar heartland.

Before the Festival, however, the South Bank was a little-loved space. During the 18th and early 19th centuries the area was home to wharves, warehouses, factories and breweries, all making use of the river frontage but also suffering from occasional flooding. During the late 18th century the Albert Embankment was built close by, helping to stabilize the southern banks between Vauxhall and Lambeth, yet the project stopped short of the South Bank.

The area was shaped further – or misshaped – by the arrival of the railways, with multiple lines carved through the streets of Georgian and Victorian terraces, as well as pushing their way across the Thames. The legacy of the railways is still ever present here, seen not just at nearby stations such as Waterloo, Charing Cross, Blackfriars and London Bridge, but also visible within the complex network of arterial viaducts and cuttings, as well as the river crossings. The South Bank itself is interrupted by the Hungerford Railway Bridge, which heads over the river to Charing Cross. The 1864 railway crossing, designed by John Hawkshaw, controversially replaced a former suspension footbridge here designed by Isambard Kingdom Brunel, with the gesture of a walkway added alongside the railway crossing offering some small compensation to pedestrians.[2]

The transformation of the South Bank really began during the early 20th century with the arrival of the London County Council (LCC). The LCC was first established in 1889 and originally based at Spring Gardens, in St James', within the home of the former Metropolitan Board of Works. But as the LCC began to grow and take on new responsibilities, as well as staff, it was clear that a new and purpose-built headquarters would be needed. After much debate, the LCC agreed to buy a large site on the south of the river, which had formerly been home to flour mills, workshops and factories.

Part of the intention of choosing a site on the 'wrong side of the river' was to stimulate growth in Lambeth, with recognition that the area was in need of regeneration. Situated right alongside Westminster Bridge, which had been rebuilt in the 1860s, the site was also close to the Palace of Westminster and the Houses of Parliament, with a tram line linking the two sides of the river all the way up to 1952.

ABOVE The former offices at Sea Containers now serve as a luxury hotel, while the OXO Tower can be seen to the right. Seifert's King's Reach office tower has been converted into an apartment building.

Architect Ralph Knott won the commission to design the principal, six-storey block of County Hall in an 'Edwardian baroque' style, with the imposing design embracing the riverside setting. Construction began in 1911 with completion in 1922, when the building was officially opened by King George V. Barely a decade later, it was clear that more space was needed and two additional blocks were added, completed in 1939, while County Hall was designated a Grade II* listed building in 1951.

Much as intended, County Hall eventually became a catalyst for the revival of the South Bank. As the LCC itself evolved, the centre of gravity shifted southwards with not just politicians but planners, architects and urbanists all drawn to their County Hall offices and to the South Bank. Like so much of London, the area suffered significant damage from wartime bombing, but by the early Forties the South Bank had also been earmarked by the LCC itself as a potential site for the development of new cultural institutions for the capital.

Patrick Abercrombie and J.H. Forshaw's *County of London Plan*, commissioned by the LCC and completed in 1943, suggested removing the 'semi-derelict' riverside wharves and warehouses along the South Bank and replacing them with 'a great cultural centre' that might include a new theatre, a concert hall and the 'headquarters of various organizations'. That same year, the Royal Society of Arts first suggested the idea of a festival to celebrate the centenary of the Great Exhibition of 1851, an idea taken up and supported by newspaper editor Gerald Barry, who promoted the idea in the pages of his *News Chronicle* two years later in an open letter to the then president of the Board of Trade, Stafford Cripps; Barry would later become director general of the Festival of Britain.

Over the following years, these various ambitions overlapped and intertwined. The LCC held on to the idea, or ideal, of the South Bank as London's new cultural campus, with the Royal Festival Hall forming the first and most important element of a bespoke collection of venues. But around this there was the wider idea of a truly national celebration, with the South Bank serving as the focal point for a dedicated assembly of pavilions celebrating Britain's national identity, while symbolizing post-war recovery and also looking forward to the future, in a similar way to the Great Exhibition of 1851. In this way, this once neglected part of the Thames became a kind of dreamland, where the hopes and ambitions of a growing number of politicians, planners, architects, designers and artists began to coalesce and combine.

Despite its many advantages, central location and riverside setting, the South Bank site still presented many challenges. One of the first and most important tasks was to stabilize the riverbank itself, with the creation of a new river wall along the southern shore of the Thames, which helped to reclaim an extra 1.8 hectares (4.5 acres) of land. 'It has quite transformed the familiar patchwork of rubble and half-derelict

ABOVE The OXO Tower is now home to a blend of apartments, restaurants and retail, all adding to the increasingly cosmopolitan mix on the South Bank.

buildings which had for so long monopolized the prospect from the South Bank,' wrote Ian Cox in the official guide book to the Festival of Britain's South Bank Exhibition: 'One of the principal aims of the Festival is to bring to the British way of life some enrichment that will endure for long after the Festival is over. It is fitting, therefore, that the main national Exhibition should be the first occupant of a site which has been so long abandoned by human enterprise and so newly won from the river.'[3]

Beyond this, the 11-hectare (27-acre) Festival site was intersected by both the Hungerford Bridge and the Waterloo Bridge, which was rebuilt in 1945, while the outer edges of the South Bank could be said to be defined by Westminster Bridge to the south-west and Blackfriars Bridge to the east. Along the river frontage itself, as old photographs and models from the Forties suggest, there were the remnants of the old wharves and warehouses interspersed with open patches of ground. Of the few remaining buildings, the most prominent and elegant was the old Lion Brewery building, which had been damaged by a combination of fire and wartime bombing. The brewery building was demolished to make way for the Royal Festival Hall, along with any other remaining structures on the site. The one notable exception, however, was the Shot Tower, which originally formed part of a lead-making factory. While the buildings around its base were removed, the tower itself was retained for the duration of the Festival and was repurposed by Hugh Casson, the Festival's director of architecture, as a lighthouse, or beacon, overlooking the pavilions of the South Bank Exhibition and marking the way to an event that still resonates down through the ages.

ABOVE The public spaces and 'outdoor rooms' of the South Bank are a vital ingredient here, as seen in the plaza between the BFI Southbank and the National Theatre.

FESTIVAL OF BRITAIN

The Festival of Britain was a unique undertaking with a character all of its own. While there was talk, in the early days, of an international trade fair the Festival gradually transformed into something more specific and celebratory, aimed at the people of Britain itself rather than an international audience. In this respect and many others, the Festival was very different to the World Fairs and expositions that flourished during the mid-century period, including the Brussels World's Fair of 1958.

The 1951 pavilions and exhibits were focused primarily on Britain rather than seeking participation from other countries. Given the growing importance of the post-war independence movement, the theme of the Commonwealth was also treated carefully, with the focus remaining on the home nations.[4] The Festival marked the centenary of the Great Exhibition, with one dedicated pavilion devoted to 'recalling' the Crystal Palace. Yet the guiding idea was that the Festival, particularly the South Bank Exhibition, should convey a broader and more ambitious narrative.

'What the visitor will see on the South Bank is an attempt at something new in exhibitions – a series of sequences of things to look at, arranged in a particular order so as to tell one continuous, interwoven story,' wrote Ian Cox in the Exhibition guide book. 'The order is important. For the South Bank Exhibition is neither a museum of British culture nor a trade show of British wares; it tells the story of British contributions to world civilizations in the arts of peace. That story has a beginning, a middle and an end – even if that end consists of nothing more final than fingerposts into the future.'[5]

The South Bank Exhibition formed the principal element within the Festival as a whole, gathering in over eight million visitors during the summer of 1951. The Festival of Britain was fully funded by Clement Attlee's Labour government and championed by Herbert Morrison, who was Leader of the House of Commons, as well as Lord President of the Privy Council, deputy

RIGHT An aerial view of the South Bank Exhibition site shows the circular Dome of Discovery, the Royal Festival Hall and the pavilions arranged around them.

leader of the Labour Party and briefly held the post of Foreign Secretary in 1951. Morrison had also served as the leader of the LCC for six years during the Thirties and retained close links with the LCC, which supported the Festival and was closely involved with the South Bank site alongside County Hall. But Morrison was always careful to try and avoid an overt political dimension to the Festival, looking to focus instead on arts and culture, as well as science and progress.

Morrison appointed another champion of the idea, the newspaper editor Gerald Barry, to serve as director general of the Festival of Britain and established an advisory Festival Council and a Festival of Britain Office, which was a fully funded government department in its own right. Various other organizations were also asked to advise the Festival Office, including the Arts Council, the Council of Industrial Design and the British Film Institute (BFI), which was established in 1933 and then government funded from 1949, making its home on the South Bank from 1951 onwards.

As neither a politician nor a government man, Barry was determined to ensure that the Festival was seen as something distinct and separate from the Labour government, which was slowly losing momentum and popularity during the late Forties. Barry began making his own appointments, as he sought to build a dedicated team to design and deliver the Festival and the South Bank Exhibition in particular, which would form the most complex and ambitious part of the whole enterprise.

One of Barry's most important choices was Hugh Casson, who was appointed director of architecture for the South Bank Exhibition. An

ABOVE The Royal Festival Hall was the only permanent, legacy building included in the South Bank Exhibition.

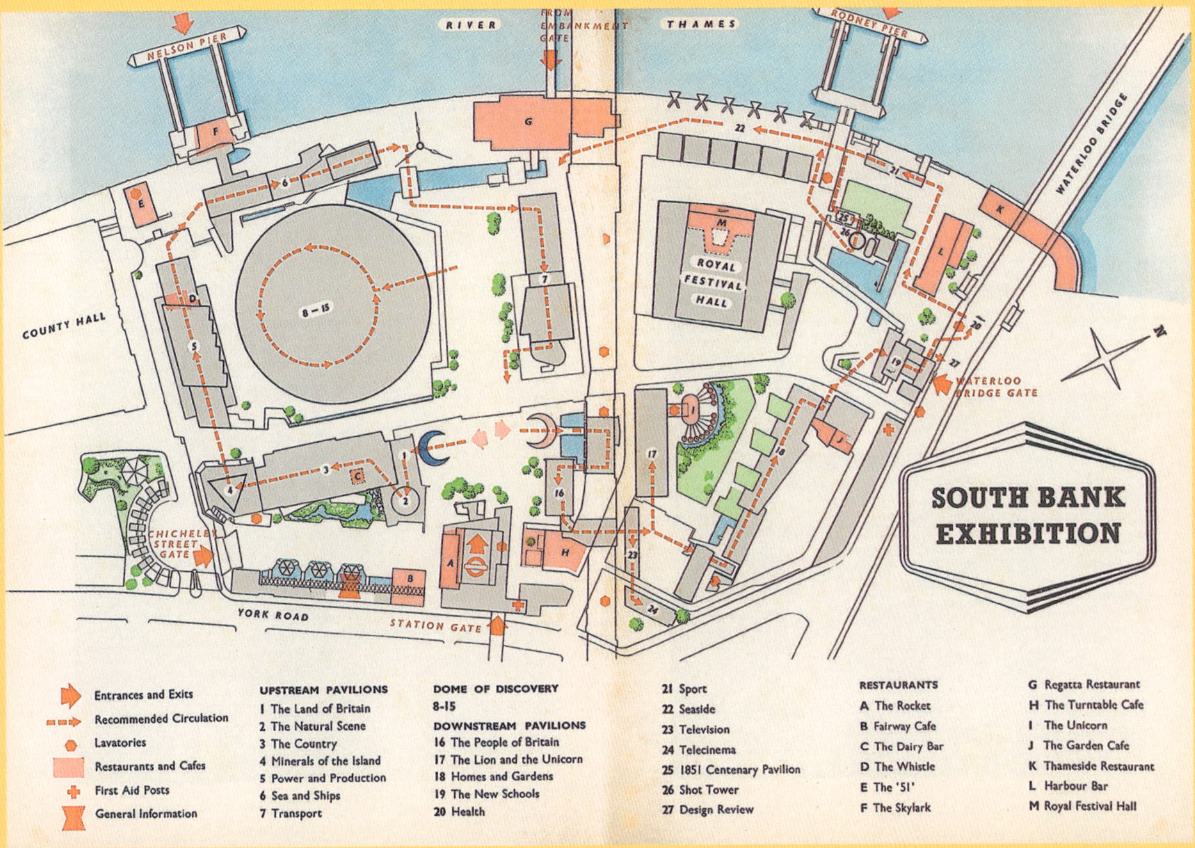

architect, writer and illustrator, Casson had studied at Cambridge, the Bartlett School of Architecture and the British School in Athens. During World War II Casson worked in the camouflage unit of the Air Ministry and was still in his thirties when he was appointed to his Festival role in 1948. In his journalism and writing, Casson had established himself as a modernist and was well connected both socially and professionally with architects, designers and artists who took a broadly modernist and forward-looking approach. The team that Casson began building around him was mostly of a similar age and outlook, including the members of his 'Design Group', an influential inner circle that consisted of Misha Black, Ralph Tubbs, James Gardner and James Holland, as well as Casson himself.

'The temporary life of the Exhibition encouraged every sort of experiment,' said Casson,[6] who was open to new ideas, as well as the use of fresh materials and innovative structural engineering. Given that all the

TOP A map of the Exhibition offers suggested circulation routes through the site and around the pavilions.
ABOVE The Exhibition was devoted to history, progress and pleasure, with a choice of restaurants and cafés.

pavilions and other Festival structures at the South Bank were intended to last little more than a year, with the important exception of the Royal Festival Hall (see page 38), there was a liberating aspect to the programme, with architects such as Tubbs, Basil Spence, H.T. Cadbury-Brown and others taking Casson's lead and adopting an approach that was often experimental but also exuberant and, at times, playful.

'We were all really between 30 and 40 with absolutely no experience,' Casson said. 'The last five years everybody had been doing something else in the war. None of us had ever built anything, none of us had ever organized anything, except Misha Black, who'd organized travelling exhibitions to buy more Spitfires… Our little designer group was set to find a place to have this exhibition, and then get out a sort of synopsis of what it should contain and how it would be put over…'[7]

Morrison and Barry steered Casson and his Design Group towards the South Bank site, which they instantly embraced: 'We thought this was absolutely perfect. It had the most wonderful view, from Big Ben to St Paul's. It had the river as one boundary. It had… opportunities for river steamers. It had a tube at Waterloo and a tube at Charing Cross, buses surrounding the site in all directions so all the crowds could get there and away, easily. It was bang central and it wasn't too big.'[8]

The LCC committed to the development of the Royal Festival Hall, designed by an in-house team led by Robert Matthew and Leslie Martin, on the understanding that the building would not only be the major performance venue for the Festival itself but would form the starting point for the LCC's future ambitions for the South Bank. The various 'upstream' and 'downstream' pavilions designed under Casson's direction would then be arranged around the Festival Hall, sitting within a segment of land defined by the river to the north, York Road to the south, County Hall to the west and Waterloo Bridge to the east, while the Hungerford Railway Bridge acted to divide the Festival site into smaller segments. Two river piers – the Nelson Pier and the Rodney Pier – were positioned either side of the Hungerford Bridge, while a series of screens were set up along the border of York Road to further control and contain what was to become a miniature town or Festival village during the summer of 1951, complete with its own bars, cafés and restaurants.

The Piers took passengers up to the Festival Pleasure Gardens at Battersea Park, which offered a completely different experience. Here, visitors could enjoy a miniature railway, a Big Dipper and other fairground rides, as well as a wine garden and a riverside restaurant, with James Gardner playing the role of chief designer here. A Festival ship, the *Campania*, was borrowed from the Admiralty and designer James Holland entrusted with converting the escort carrier into 'a floating fairground', which offered a miniature version of the South Bank experience, travelling around the British coast during the summer of 1951 and docking at key ports.

There were many other events, exhibitions and arts festivals right across Britain during 1951, all falling under the umbrella of the Festival of Britain. In London, there was also a science show in South Kensington and a 'live architecture' exhibition devoted to housing and town planning in Poplar, supported by the LCC and featuring contributions from two eminent modernist architects, Frederick Gibberd and F.R.S. Yorke. Yet it was the South Bank Exhibition, above all, which caught the public's imagination and offered an almost utopian vision to a tired city, worn out by war and austerity. Through its own architecture and design, the Exhibition and its 'interwoven story' sought to remind visitors of the best of Britain while holding out the promise of a brighter future.

OPPOSITE The design of the South Bank Exhibition made the most of the riverside setting, including the provision of two working passenger piers.

FESTIVAL HALL
PIER & BOATS

FESTIVAL ARCHITECTURE

The design and delivery of the many elements that made up the South Bank Exhibition, for the 1951 Festival of Britain, was challenging in many different respects. The whole project was a race against time, with Hugh Casson and his Design Group given little more than two years to masterplan, commission, create and build a temporary town on the banks of the Thames. Each of the 27 pavilions within this town formed a chapter in 'the story of British contributions to world civilization' and was set within a carefully ordered route, which started at the main site entrance on York Road and began with the upstream pavilions (devoted to the 'Land of Britain') on one side of Hungerford Bridge and continued with the downstream pavilions (devoted to the 'People of Britain') on the other side, while also wrapping their way around the new Royal Festival Hall (see page 38).

Although the various pavilions came under the overall direction of the Design Group, with its five members taking on direct authorship of a handful of them, each building required a dedicated team of its own, which generally included an architect, a 'theme convener' and display designers. In some cases these roles overlapped yet the larger, more complex pavilions sometimes required more contributors and engineers. Each building needed to have its own character and identity, even if there were certain similarities at times in the design vocabulary and choice of materials, with steelwork widely used on account of its 'speedy erection and dismantling', according to Casson, and 'pre-cast concrete units preferred to the complications of shuttering'. 'Wood, the most useful and versatile of materials, was desperately short and had, alas, to be avoided as far as possible.'[9]

The Design Group agreed that 'every attempt should be made to find and commission young and untried talent', with most of the selected architects in their thirties or forties. 'We chose them for their honesty of aim and sympathy of viewpoint,' said Casson. 'They all spoke the

RIGHT The Festival Hall was the lynchpin of the South Bank Exhibition and its permanent landmark, while the base of the Shot Tower can be seen in the background.

3/7/51

These diagrams show what happens when violinist, tympanist and singer emit a note at the same instant. Approximately one-tenth of a second later the sound waves have reached the strong yellow, red and blue lines respectively (many minor reflections have been omitted). A rich tone is achieved by hearing a large number of separate reflections so that the ear accepts them as a single sound.

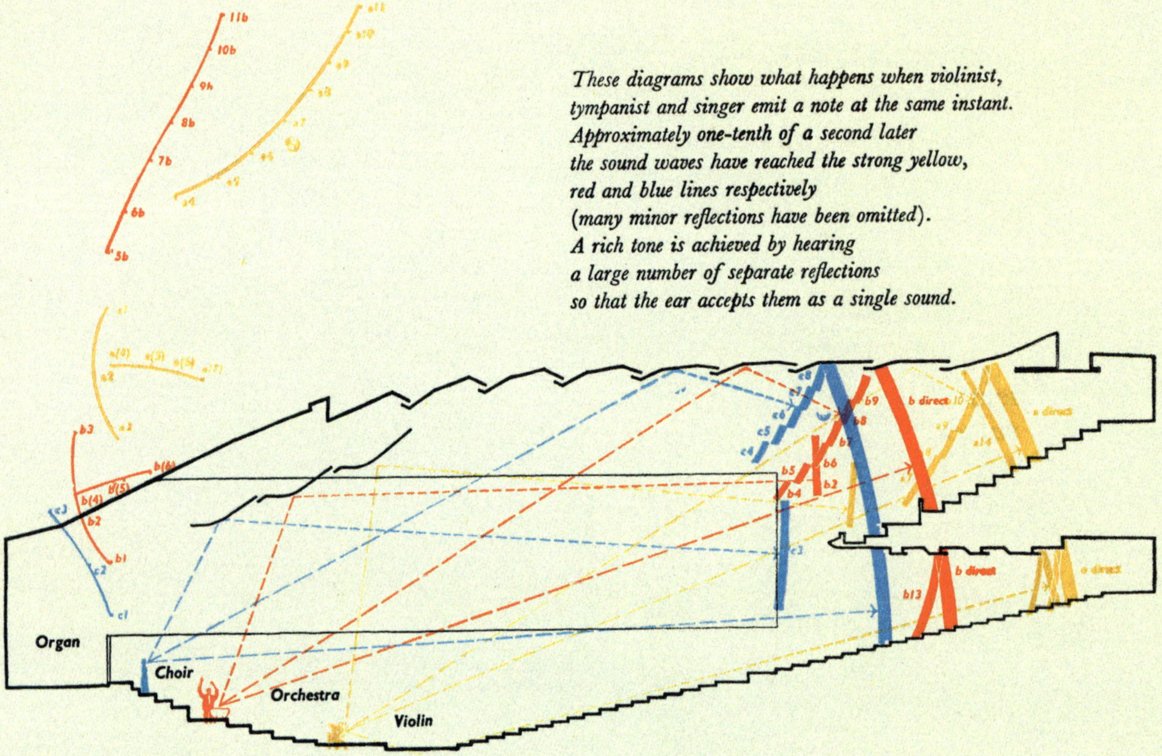

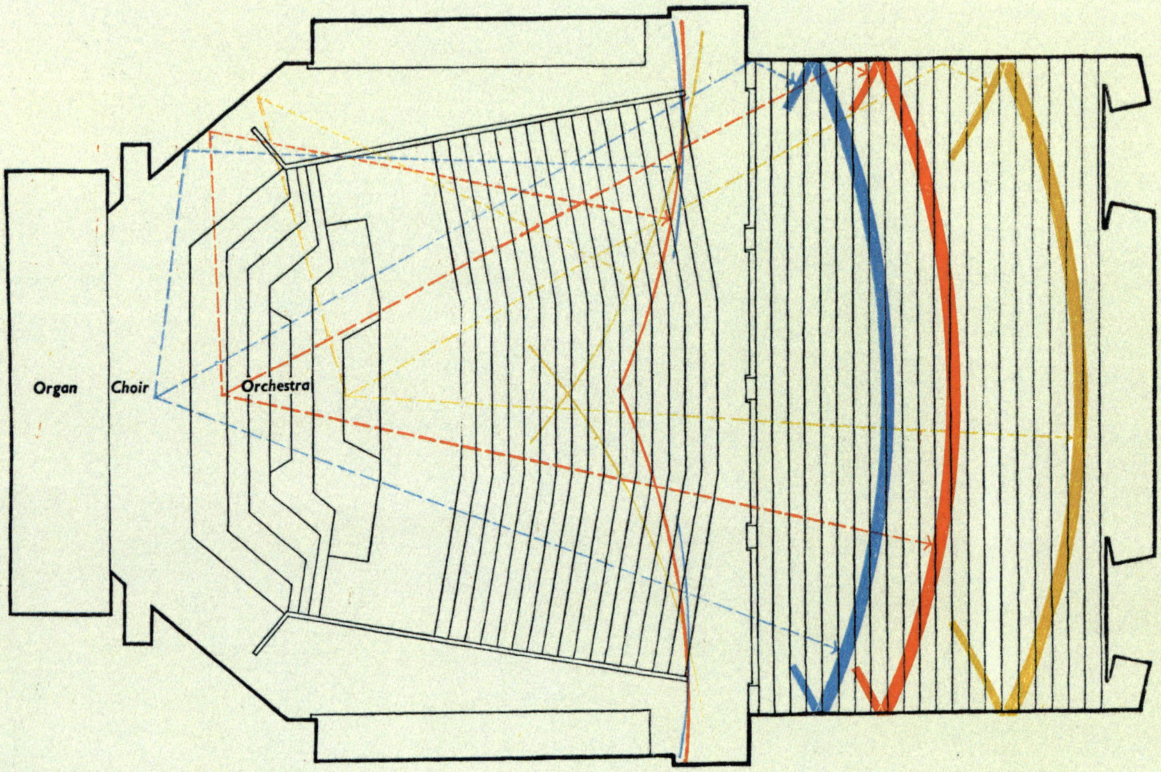

same language but each with enough variety of intonation to make it interesting.'[10] Chosen architects included H.T. Cadbury-Brown, Brian O'Rorke and Basil Spence, while the more established architect Wells Coates, who designed the influential Isokon apartment building (1934) in London's Belsize Park, was entrusted with the design of the Television pavilion and the Telecinema, hosted by the British Film Institute. Casson himself designed the 1851 Centenary pavilion and the Shot Tower, which was already on the site and was repurposed as 'a modern lighthouse with a double flashing beam welcoming visitors as far as 45 miles [72 km] away'.[11]

Spence's Sea & Ships pavilion was one of the most eye-catching structures on the site, sitting right next to the riverbank and alongside the Nelson Pier. Apart from his contributions to a small number of residential projects, Spence's previous experience at the time was mostly in exhibition design, including the ICI pavilion at the 1938 Empire Exhibition in Glasgow as well as contributions to the Britain Can Make It exhibition of 1946. Given Britain's status as a seafaring nation, its shipbuilding tradition and the Thames-side setting, the Sea & Ships pavilion was an important ingredient for the Exhibition as a whole, holding the massive sterns of a passenger liner, a whale factory ship and an oil tanker: 'The central exhibit is a model of a floating dock, containing a modern liner', while 'around this are examples of twenty-four different vessels, all specialized for a particular kind of duty'.[12]

Running parallel to the river, with various shifts in level, the building offered a journey in itself from the days of the sailing ships, through marine engines, propellers, shipbuilding and fishing until visitors arrived at the floating dock at the far end. 'A giant framework of steel towers and gantries tied the composition together' and 'the overall effect was more deconstruction than construction, Spence capturing the spirit of a modern shipyard scene with its essays in incompleteness'.[13]

OPPOSITE The acoustics of the Royal Festival Hall's auditorium were carefully conceived but later refined.
ABOVE The architecture and appearance of the Festival Hall has also been refined over time, while carefully conserving the essential character of the building.

The largest and, arguably, most dramatic building on the South Bank Festival site was the Dome of Discovery, which hosted eight individual pavilions under its giant, curving roof. The idea of a superdome had been settled by the Design Group at an early stage, providing a centrepiece for the Exhibition at a size and scale comparable with only the Royal Festival Hall on the opposite side of the site. The ambition was for the largest dome in the world to date, at 111m (365ft) in diameter, while the futuristic, saucer-like form spoke of modernity in itself.

Designed by Ralph Tubbs from the Design Group, the Dome of Discovery was an innovative precursor of Greenwich Peninsula's Millennium Dome, designed by Richard Rogers and Mike Davies. The design allowed for pavilions at ground level but also within a series of mezzanines, with one of these devoted to outer space and featuring a collection of telescopes. Given the experimental character of Tubbs' building, working out how to build it offered another challenge for Festival engineers, Freeman Fox & Partners.

'The geodetic triangular rib structure and smooth metal cover was to be made of aluminium alloy, a material we'd never designed on this scale before,' wrote engineer Ralph Freeman, 'and the ribs were to thrust on to an all-welded steel box ring girder, itself held aloft 40 feet [12m] above ground by a series of slender lattice steel masts leaning inwards and forming a complete triangulated support system all round the ring.'[14] Again, the design, engineering and completion of the Dome was a race against time, with Tubbs and Freeman, Fox & Partners working closely together to find the right structural solutions.

The building was undoubtedly Tubbs' masterpiece and, as fellow Design Group member Misha Black described it, 'a magnificent awe-inspiring interior space designed with great sensitivity'. It was however, admitted Black, a shame that so much exhibition content was then loaded into the space, undermining the drama of the superdome itself:

'The Dome of Discovery was at its most dramatic when empty, when on a bitterly cold evening in the winter of 1950 all the workmen on the site were invited to a celebratory meal, the roofs having been finally battened down on all the buildings... The speeches of exhortation to greater effort and fewer trade-union disputes were dreary and misconceived. The atmosphere became frigid as the night when suddenly one man sent his paper plate (food eaten) whizzing across the void. In a moment a thousand plates were spinning, until the whole volume of the Dome was alive with white discs, as though invaded by flying fish. This was a magical moment which all the skills of the exhibition designers could not emulate.'[15]

As well as hosting the Festival pavilions themselves the South Bank site also needed to cater to the various needs of over eight million people. As well as the restaurant at the Royal Festival Hall, there was a choice of 12 restaurants, bars and cafés on the site, all of which were purpose designed and built. Selected architects and designers included Leonard Manasseh, Trevor Dannatt and Misha Black, who designed the Regatta Restaurant. Nearby, Jane Drew and Maxwell Fry were commissioned to design the Riverside Restaurant underneath Waterloo Bridge, with a large mural by artist Ben Nicholson marking the entrance to the restaurant as well as works by Barbara Hepworth and Eduardo Paolozzi situated within the building. The Riverside Restaurant lasted six years rather than the initially proposed six months, but was eventually replaced by the headquarters of the British Film Institute (see page 64).

One of the most famous structures of the Festival's South Bank site was conceived through an architectural competition rather than a direct invitation. Although the timing was tight for every element of the Festival site, Casson and his Design Group agreed that there should be some attempt to cast the net wide and invite ideas from beyond their own circles of colleagues and contributors. So they decided to launch an architectural competition for 'a vertical feature', an emblem of the South Bank Exhibition that would be – rather like the repurposed Shot Tower – a beacon visible across the entire site and from over the river. The budget was modest and the

OPPOSITE The futuristic Skylon served as a beacon for the South Bank Exhibition but also became emblematic of the Festival as a whole; its name lives on at the principal restaurant at the Festival Hall.

purpose of the building limited in comparison with the themed pavilions, yet the competition still attracted over 150 entries. The winners were the two young architects, Philip Powell and Hidalgo Moya, who had met at the Architectural Association. Their design was a floating, cigar-shaped structure, like an airship turned upon its nose tip, which would be illuminated at night, serving as a giant lantern that marked the riverside location of the Exhibition.

Having chosen Powell & Moya's design, engineer Felix Samuely was appointed to help them build it, using a framework of steel and aluminium supported by three spider-like legs and additional supporting cables. Samuely helped to give the Skylon, as it was named via another open competition, a magical sense of lightness. Rather like the Dome of Discovery, the Skylon spoke of the future, yet it was – in its way – more visible and possessed a purity of form. Unlike the Dome, which needed to accommodate a whole host of functions and themes, the Skylon was sculptural and symbolic. Rather than appearing among the pavilions and restaurants in the Exhibition guide book, it was – instead – listed among its many artworks.

A delightful folly that seemed to encapsulate the exuberant, celebratory and more playful strand of the Festival, the Skylon certainly gripped the imagination of the visiting public. Older critics such as John Summerson may have dismissed the Skylon as 'a silly toy', but even after its removal and destruction Powell & Moya's invention has remained in the collective consciousness of the country. When Conran & Partners revived and refurbished the restaurant at the Royal Festival Hall in 2007, the name chosen for the refreshed eatery was – of course – Skylon.

THE FESTIVAL LEGACY

Although the pavilions, restaurants and cafés of the South Bank Exhibition of 1951 were intended to be temporary, the impact of the Festival of Britain was wide reaching and long lasting. Importantly, the architecture and design of the Exhibition introduced a mass audience to mid-century modern architecture in a way that had not been seen in Britain before. Rather than the pure and sometimes didactic modernism of the pre-war period, Hugh Casson and his team projected a more friendly and accessible version that managed to entice and entrance many of the eight million plus visitors, while winning over many sceptics.

Given the numbers involved and the intensely high-profile nature of the Exhibition and the Festival as a whole, the impact of such exposure should not be neglected. There was talk, for a time, of the 'Festival Style', which was – for the most part – a variant of expressive, mid-century modernism with a British twist to it. There was a touch of eccentricity and a sometimes whimsical strand to the Festival Style, as seen in follies such as the Skylon, yet at the same time the South Bank Exhibition offered the most complete and rounded statement of post-war modernism seen in Britain up to that point. Rather than offering a sanitized version of modernist architecture, the Exhibition offered colour, texture and delight, suggesting that modern design could make the world a better and more interesting place while doing so with warmth.

There may have been some truth in critic Reyner Banham's assertion that the Exhibition simply saw Britain doing some 'catching up' with many other European nations and particularly with America. But for such a conservative and damaged country, this process of catching up was vital in itself. It helped to open a door, encouraging greater openness towards modern architecture with tangible results seen right across the country. The LCC's role in supporting the event, as well as designing the Royal Festival Hall in the International Style, was also important, with the LCC and many other

RIGHT The Royal Festival Hall was the most accomplished British interpretation of the International Style up to that point.

ROYAL FESTIVAL HALL

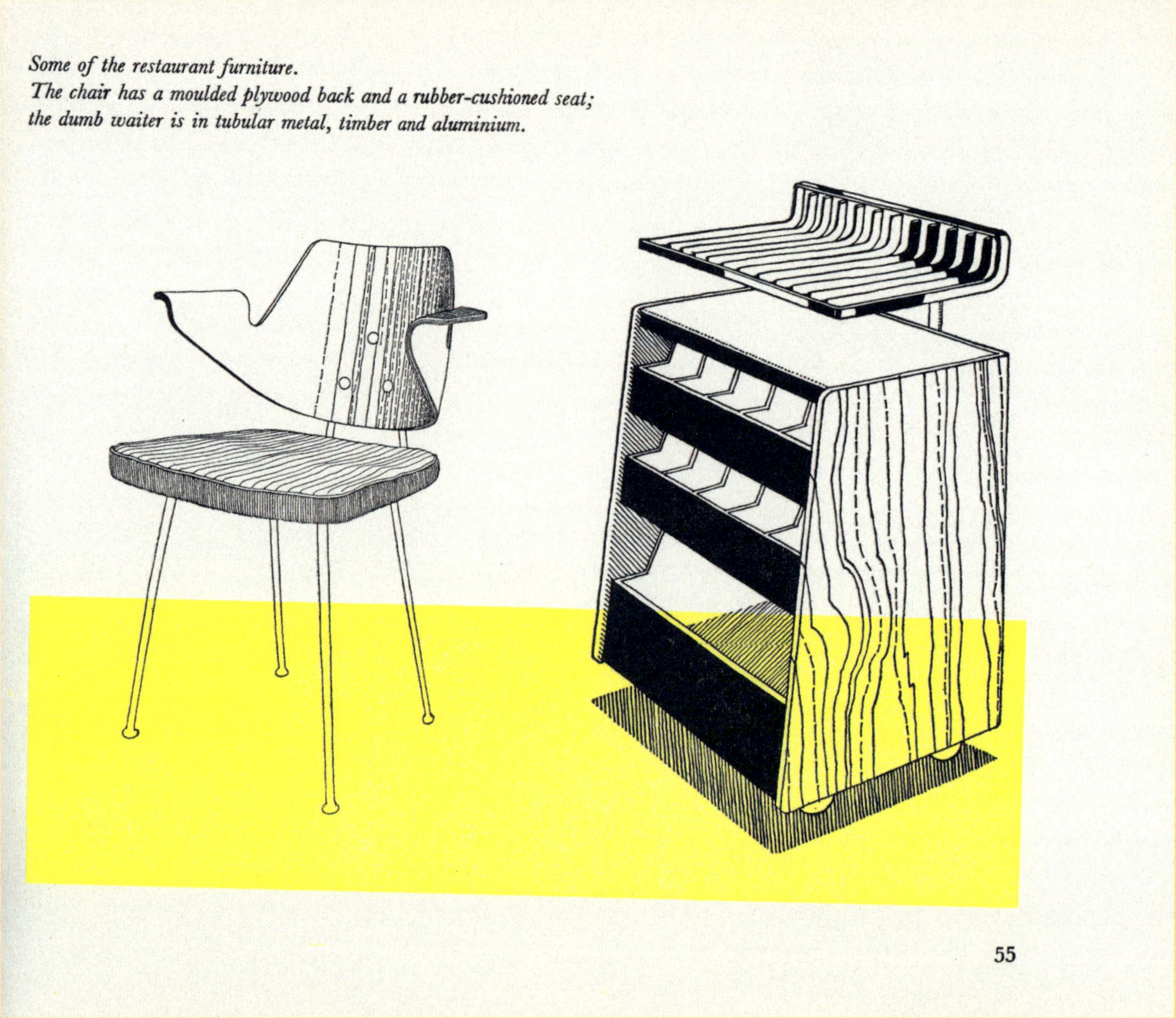

council planning departments increasingly adopting modernist principles and solutions as the post-war reconstruction and revival process accelerated.

Not everyone came out in support of the Festival of Britain, of course, nor the South Bank Exhibition, but there were many notable admirers, including many commentators within the national press who were eventually won round and significant voices within the world of architecture itself. The *Architectural Review*, for example, was positively effusive, suggesting that the South Bank Exhibition was 'a triumphant demonstration of the vitality of contemporary British architecture': 'It is clear to all those who have followed the modern movement in architecture, and who comprehend the ideas for the future still only implicit in it, that at the South Bank exhibition we have not only a major architectural event but a work of art which – like the Crystal Palace before it – has potential world-wide influence.'[16]

For the *Architectural Review* and its editors, one of the greatest successes of the South Bank Exhibition was its planning, with all of the lessons implicit in the creation of what was – in effect – 'a new town'. Here, the public realm was just as important as the buildings and pavilions themselves, with a pleasing balance between inside and outside space. People were put first, rather than cars, with an inviting promenade established alongside the river and the provision

ABOVE The interiors of the Royal Festival Hall featured an innovative collection of furniture, largely designed by Robin Day.

of gardens and outdoor rooms seen as an integral part of the overall plan of this temporary town by the Thames. There were, said the *Architectural Review*, many points of inspiration here for our urban planners. Reyner Banham, who was clearly suspicious of the 'mythology' around the seminal influence of the 'Festival Style', agreed that the greatest legacy of the South Bank Exhibition was the imaginative, sensitive character of the landscaping and its urban plan:

'If one tries to recall the experience of the South Bank as an inhabited environment, if one looks at the backgrounds to the family snaps and the surviving footages of film, the landscaping is omnipresent in a way that it was not at any other great expo… Of all that was designed and done, it was one of the great triumphs of imaginative professional skill at the Festival. It was probably more truly English and more genuinely innovating than much else that was more loudly praised at the time and more thoroughly forgotten since.'[17]

Although some architects later turned their backs on the Festival of Britain, it is true that the South Bank Exhibition offered an important catalyst for the careers of many of the architects and designers involved. They included Hugh Casson himself, as well as Basil Spence, H.T. Cadbury-Brown, Ralph Tubbs, Powell & Moya and many others who had little opportunity before the Festival of Britain to build at any significant size or scale. The Festival was an

ABOVE Architect Peter Moro was put in charge of the interiors of the Festival Hall, leading a dedicated team while also designing many elements himself, including the 'Net & Ball' patterned carpets.

extraordinary opportunity for many of them and, even if so much of their work was later swept away, it had been witnessed by millions and documented in multiple mediums, becoming part of the Festival 'mythology'.

For the South Bank itself the Exhibition was also transformative. Although much of the Festival site was cleared after the 1951 Exhibition, the riverside promenade remained in place and became a much loved public space in its own right. Part of the cleared site between County Hall and Royal Festival Hall was used as a car park but in 1977 this was then transformed into Jubilee Gardens, another valuable communal amenity space, with the London Eye eventually placed between the park and the river in the year of the millennium.

Designed by architects David Marks and Julia Barfield, the London Eye – or Millennium Wheel – sat perfectly within the spirit of architectural experimentation first established here by the Festival and the South Bank Exhibition. Rather like the Skylon, the London Eye is a vertical landmark rising on the riverbank, but upon an epic scale. The combination of verticality and the form of the wheel to create a unique observatory overlooking the South Bank, the Thames and the cityscape beyond was an inspired but highly experimental idea in its own right, offering a completely new perspective on central London.

'Architecture and engineering are two sides of the same coin for us,' said architect David Marks. 'And I suppose the idea of being above everything is inherent in all of us. How many of us have never dreamt of flying at a young age? I don't know where it comes from but it seems to be in our DNA that we love a view from above. It appeals to your intellect because you are trying to make the connections with your experiences on the ground, as everything looks so different from above, and secondly there's just the sheer beauty of it and those things are inherently appealing to us. It is absolutely thrilling.'[18]

Similarly, the Dome of Discovery, the Skylon and other Festival structures were imaginative fusions of architecture and engineering. There was a powerful multi-disciplinary strand to the South Bank Exhibition overall, with the collaborative programme including designers of all kinds, landscape architects, as well as artists and sculptors. The creative relationship between modern artists and architects was clearly established and underlined at the Exhibition, which featured artworks by John Piper, Henry Moore, Lynn Chadwick, Barbara Hepworth, Jacob Epstein and many others. This relationship continued to flourish along the South Bank over subsequent decades, as seen in the profusion of public artworks along the river, including Frank Dobson's 'London Pride' (1951) situated outside the National Theatre, William Pye's 'Zemran' (1971) on the upper terrace of the Queen's Walk, outside Queen Elizabeth Hall, and Ian Walters' bust of Nelson Mandela (1982) outside the Royal Festival Hall.

The Royal Festival Hall itself was, of course, one of the greatest legacies of the South Bank Exhibition. This was the one surviving landmark building of the Festival, forming the starting point for a series of major cultural institutions running along the southern shore of the Thames, explored in more detail over the following pages. This was, as envisaged back in the early Forties, the beginning of a new campus of the arts, which gradually took shape over the course of the Fifties, Sixties and Seventies. While the South Bank Exhibition was completed against the clock, the subsequent buildings took 25 years to complete. But this journey through architecture and time is also part of the fascination of this very special segment of London.

OPPOSITE The gardens and outdoor spaces of the Exhibition provided opportunities to rest and relax, with outdoor seating specially designed by Ernest Race.

THE BUILDINGS

ROYAL FESTIVAL HALL

Leslie Martin,
Robert Matthew,
Peter Moro et al,
1951

INTRODUCTION

The official guide book to the 1951 Festival of Britain suggests that its showcase South Bank concert hall 'can claim to be a work of art in itself'.[19] For many visitors to the Royal Festival Hall, both then and now, this is not an exaggeration. It is one of Britain's most adventurous and innovative post-war public buildings, designed within a sophisticated modernist aesthetic, yet it managed to instantly seduce audiences while avoiding some of the criticisms levelled at certain mid-century contemporaries, as well as later additions to the South Bank. As a new performance space, with seating for around 3,000 people, it was widely regarded as a masterpiece, meeting its remit 'as an example of modern English architecture at its best, and as a well-tuned instrument for orchestras and conductors of international repute'.[20]

The success of the Royal Festival Hall and its status as a landmark concert hall is all the more

RIGHT The Royal Festival Hall remains the lynchpin of a vibrant riverside neighbourhood that continues to evolve and grow.

remarkable given the multiple challenges and constraints involved in its design and construction. Like the Festival of Britain itself, which took place around it, the Festival Hall was conceived and constructed against the clock. Yet, unlike all of the temporary exhibition pavilions that surrounded it on the southern shore of the Thames, the Festival Hall was always intended to be a permanent and long-lasting structure, forming the foundation of a new campus of the arts. Not only was the conception and completion of the building itself a race against time, but it was also built to a tightly controlled budget of £2 million at a time of continuing post-war austerity, when many building materials were still in short supply. And, although it offered important advantages, the riverside site itself needed to be stabilized with a new river wall, while remaining buildings on the site, such as the old Lion Brewery, were cleared away.

Given all of these considerations, it was extraordinary how accomplished the resulting building was in almost every respect. Outwardly, the building was a sophisticated exemplar of the International Style, yet its detailing was always elegant and – at times – expressive, with the gentle curve of its riverside façade softening the largely linear outline. Inside, the level of refinement of so many bespoke ingredients and the characterful quality of the auditorium, in particular, were striking and much praised. Over the decades there have been adjustments, alterations and updates to the Royal Festival Hall, yet the unique personality of this landmark building has been respected and retained, ensuring that it remains a much loved focal point for the South Bank.

ABOVE & OPPOSITE Art and sculpture have always played an important role in and around the Festival Hall, including Ian Walters' *Nelson Mandela* statue (1982), above, and Reg Butler's *Birdcage* (1951), opposite.

SOUTHBANK CENTRE

ROYAL FESTIVAL HALL

CONTEXT

While the 1951 South Bank Exhibition as a whole came under the remit of the Festival of Britain's director of architecture, Hugh Casson, and his team, the Royal Festival Hall was an exception. The concert hall project was run instead by the department of architecture at London County Council (LCC), headed by Robert Matthew and based at nearby County Hall. The LCC saw the Festival Hall as the first step in meeting their ambition of creating an original collection of new cultural institutions on the South Bank site and embraced the challenge of having the building ready in time for the Festival deadline, while also taking responsibility for its future running and long term upkeep.

Robert Matthew began drawing together a dedicated team to work on the Royal Festival Hall, with his role compared to that of a conductor leading an orchestra. In the autumn of 1948 he appointed architect Leslie Martin to serve as his deputy and to lead the Festival Hall design team, with Martin usually credited as the chief creative force behind the building. Martin had just turned 30 and, after teaching at the University of Hull, had spent much of the war overseeing the reconstruction of railway stations and vital infrastructure. This wartime service meant that Martin had experience of meeting complex logistical challenges yet he was also an intellectual, creative modernist with a love of the arts, making him well suited to his new post as Festival Hall team leader.

Another key member of the LCC group was architect Peter Moro, who was given responsibility for the interiors of the building. Born in Germany and partly educated in Switzerland, Moro had settled in England in 1936, working initially with Berthold Lubetkin's Tecton and then becoming an influential tutor at the Regent Street Polytechnic, with a number of his former students later drafted into the LCC's architecture department. He was well connected with the design world in general, helping to draw in other Festival Hall contributors such as the furniture designer Robin Day. Other members of the design team included Trevor Dannatt and the acoustics expert Hope Bagenal, while an experienced LCC architect, Edwin Williams, was in charge of managing the site and logistical planning.

OPPOSITE & ABOVE Colour, pattern and detailing all played an important part in the architectural design of the Festival Hall, as seen in its tilework, carpets and elegant wooden panelling.

DESIGN

The design of the Festival Hall was influenced by a number of factors and key concerns. Above all, the building needed to provide a state of the art concert hall capable of seating a large audience and hosting major events, including the opening programme for the Festival of Britain. A secondary performance space was also included in the original brief, but pressures on space within a constrained site inside the South Bank's Festival quadrant meant that this was put on hold. The riverside location was, of course, another key consideration with the need to connect the building to the riverside setting and provide connections with the surroundings, partly through the provision of terraces and outdoor spaces around the Festival Hall. Importantly, there was the sense from the start that this was a communal building – or 'people's palace' – and that, as well as the auditorium, it should offer other amenities, including restaurants and meeting places. The building also needed to be able to serve the practical needs of both orchestras and performers, as well as thousands of visitors, requiring functional service spaces and clear circulation routes. Beyond this, the Festival Hall was the centrepiece of a national celebration and needed to be in tune with the celebratory tone of the Festival of Britain as well as its optimistic, forward-looking narrative.

The design developed by Martin, Matthew and the LCC team has been summed up as the 'egg in the box' solution. Martin proposed floating the oval-shaped auditorium within the more or less linear outline of the building, using the spaces around the concert hall as an extra acoustic buffer that would help protect performances from any outside interference from crowds or passing trains running over nearby Hungerford Bridge. All the other ingredients of the building could then be arranged around the central auditorium over multiple levels.

'The two entrance levels at the sides could be connected by a large foyer space which, with its associated restaurants, would occupy the site area,' said Martin. 'The auditorium with its

RIGHT The organ in the auditorium, which has recently been restored, was designed by Ralph Downes and built by Harrison & Harrison.

heavy enclosing structure could be placed centrally over this within the main volume of surrounding foyers and galleries. And however incompletely it was realized, it was this central idea that provides the building with one of its main architectural attributes: the great sense of space that is opened out within the building, the flowing circulation from the symmetrically placed staircases and galleries which give access to all parts of the auditorium, the changing spatial volumes and views that are presented from these different levels and, within and enclosed by all this, the protected mass of the auditorium itself. That was the architectural conception as it was first envisaged and which we attempted to retain.'[21]

As Martin suggests, there were many benefits to the egg in the box solution beyond enclosing and protecting the central concert hall. Clear and welcoming circulation routes were established, leading up from the lower ground level through to the main foyer at upper ground level and then continuing upwards via the sweeping staircases either side of the auditorium, leading to the front stalls, mid stalls and balcony levels of the hall, as well as the amenities and services zones arranged around the performance space. While the hall itself was carefully set within a double-skinned concrete shell, with an additional cavity between them filled with sound insulation, the surrounding stairways and other parts of the Royal Festival Hall were lifted by the rich provision of natural light and a sense of open space and volume. The connections with the river were maximized, with banks of glass looking out towards the Thames and access to the adjoining terraces at upper ground level, connecting with the riverside promenade below. In many respects, the building was highly complex yet the architectural plan offered visitors to the Festival Hall a logical and pleasing invitation, with places and spaces within and without to appreciate the relationship with the Thames and the surrounding cityscape. The upper level restaurant, in particular, offered a panorama of the river and views out across to its northern shores. Yet the central purpose of the building was never forgotten.

ABOVE & OPPOSITE Despite the dramatic size and scale of the auditorium, the design of the space still manages to convey a sense of warmth and welcome.

OVERLEAF Preparations for the London Philharmonic Orchestra rehearsals on the Royal Festival Hall stage.

'The sealed box of the auditorium is from all aspects the central core of a composition in which the surrounding foyers act as a sort of rising approach on various planes,' said LCC design team member Trevor Dannatt. 'This "shape within a shape" idea is everywhere and "exterior" and "interior" are no longer separate things but parts of the basic conception. The rest of the design, the detailing, the finishes are all turned towards emphasizing this idea – light colours, space, freedom in the outer structure and a sense of preparation for the penetration of the central element with its warm and intimate colour.'[22]

OPPOSITE & ABOVE Pattern and colour were introduced into the Festival Hall with textiles by Sadie Speight and bespoke carpets by Peter Moro, while later additions include the *Terrazzo Wall* mural by artist Bruce McLean.

DELIVERY

Given the strict deadlines involved, the attention to detail exhibited by the LCC team to both the architecture and interior design of the Royal Festival Hall was more than impressive. Leslie Martin only took up his post in the autumn of 1948, with Matthew, Martin and Moro then having to build up their team to design and deliver the project. Yet the designs were largely agreed by the spring of 1949 and in May of that year the contractors began moving on to the site. By the autumn of that same year, the site had been largely drained and excavated while the concrete supporting columns and foundations were complete, with work on the superstructure just getting underway. By the spring of 1950, the roof was largely complete and King George VI and his wife came to visit.

'The King and Queen visit the site and it is announced that the hall will be known as Royal Festival Hall,' wrote LCC team architect Jean Symons in her diary of her time on the site. 'I am impressed by the detailed questions the Queen asks, and amused at the way she holds up the official procession to chat with the workers on the site. There is a sudden shower. Instead of waiting for umbrellas, the King and Queen hurry to shelter under Waterloo Bridge with everyone else. The consternation on the faces of the police guard is a joy to behold.'[23]

By the autumn of 1950, miraculously, the exteriors of the Royal Festival Hall were mostly done, including the glazing and stone cladding for the exteriors of the concrete and steel-framed building. As well as the Portland stone for the outer coat of the building, the design team managed to secure copper sheeting to coat the roof dome of the auditorium and teak for the window surrounds for the glazing on the original riverfront façade. During late 1950, at the height of the construction process, over 900 people were working on the site.

During the winter of 1950–51, the emphasis was on completing the interiors of the Royal Festival Hall. Here, again, the LCC managed to secure materials that felt relatively refined and

RIGHT A generous provision of bars, cafés and public spaces were woven into the design of the 'people's palace' from the start.

2
GREEN SIDE
Auditorium
Doors G – N
The Clore Ballroom
Cloakroom
Exit to Southbank Centre Square

luxurious in the context of continuing post-war austerity, with Derbyshire marble tiles used to coat the outer walls of the auditorium with elm and leather for the majority of the wall panelling within. Peter Moro not only directed his own team working on the interiors but also designed many details himself, including light fittings, balustrades, music stands and the carpets on the stairs and other public areas, featuring an abstract, geometric 'Net & Ball' pattern. Moro based his original design on the patterns of visualized sound waves seen upon oscilloscopes, used for acoustic tests, with Leslie Martin reputedly then adding the repeated dot, or 'ball', to his colleague's drawings.

For the interiors of the auditorium itself, Moro worked closely with acoustic consultant Hope Bagenal, who undertook extensive studies of other major concert halls across the UK and Europe. One of Moro and Bagenal's key concerns was avoiding intrusive echoes during performances, leading to the design of a carefully concentrated orchestral stage with crafted timber

ABOVE & OPPOSITE The adoption of the 'egg in the box' central auditorium also enabled the architects to create a sequence of circulation spaces around it that are full of light and rich in connections to the surroundings.

SOUTHBANK
CENTRE
SOUTHBANK
CENTRE
SOUTHBANK
CENTRE
SOUTHBANK
CENTRE

floors, panelling and roof canopy in sycamore and birch. With the sound of the orchestra controlled and directed in this way, Moro and Bagenal agreed to then use as many absorbent materials and surfaces elsewhere in the hall to reduce echo, including the seating designed by Robin Day (who also designed seating for the restaurants and other public areas) and tapestry screens for the rear walls of the ranks of floating, sculptural boxes designed by textile artist and writer Sadie Speight, who was Leslie Martin's wife.

'There was fear that there would be too little absorption and too much reverberation, and all sorts of devices were installed which could deaden it down,' said Moro. 'Unfortunately it was exactly the opposite. The acoustics had to be enlivened… and lots of things were done. The panelling was stiffened up with additional framing behind so that the panelling did not absorb by reverberation… And the ceilings, as far as I remember, were beefed up and thickened. The other thing, of course, was the organ behind the orchestra, which is an absorbent, and although there is a device for closing it up with a sliding and folding screen, they're so proud of it they leave it open most of the time and it looks much nicer than the screen. But that doesn't help acoustically either.'[24]

While the complexity of controlling the acoustics with such a large performance space was daunting, requiring many adjustments along the way, the interiors of the auditorium itself are one of the Royal Festival Hall's greatest delights. While the exteriors of the building offer an elegant but relatively restrained interpretation of the International Style, the auditorium offers a more expressive and multi-layered version of mid-century style, full of warmth and rich in colour. It is the welcoming destination point with the journey from the South Bank and its river walk, through the hinterland of foyers and communal spaces and into this dramatic and joyful space, with its banks of crafted nesting boxes cantilevering outwards from the textural walls with their rich, organic tones.

'The greatest moment is when the scaffolding comes down and the hoardings come down and the opening is there,' Moro said. 'And the King and Queen arrived, and you were all lined up and presented, and Churchill and Attlee and everybody in politics was there, all the celebrities, for the opening ceremony and the opening concert, which Malcolm Sargent conducted…

'That was fabulous. Of course there was the royal box and that was a problem, which was quite interesting, because… royalty had to also have a suite where they have their rest room and lavatory and all the rest of it. From the suite they had to cross a bit of the foyer to get into their box. Now they must never cross with the public, it's just not on, so this was a problem which planning wise I could not solve because if you connected them you would have barred the entrance to the public boxes on that side. In the end I solved it by time planning, because royalty does not go from their suite to the box until everybody else is in their seat and the public is not allowed to leave until they have gone from the box back to their suite, so they never meet. It was the first and the last four-dimensional piece of planning I have ever done, adding time to the other three dimensions.'

There was a justifiable sense of pride among the LCC design team – including Peter Moro – with the Royal Festival Hall. It was a building of not only national but international stature, which was visited by many modernist pioneers such as Le Corbusier, Walter Gropius and Marcel Breuer, as well as earning comparison with other landmark concert halls in Europe and Scandinavia.

Writing in the May 1951 issue of *Architectural Review*, editor and critic J.M. Richards was effusive about Britain's 'first civic building to have been designed in an uncompromisingly modern style', praising Matthew, Martin and their team at the LCC:

'Dr Martin and his colleagues have achieved something without precedent in this country and with very little precedent elsewhere: a modern building – modern in the sense of owing allegiance to no other age but ours – which is also monumental.'[25]

OPPOSITE The wealth of communal space on the lower levels of the Festival Hall created opportunities for additional and more informal areas, such as the Clore Ballroom, for performances and special events.

REVISIONS

During the decades following the Festival of Britain, the Royal Festival Hall became a national treasure in its own right. In 1965 the building came under the control of the Greater London Council (GLC), the successor to the LCC, but eventually became the flagship venue of the Southbank Centre following the abolition of the GLC in 1986. It is now the home of the London Philharmonic Orchestra, the Philharmonia Orchestra and other resident orchestras, while hosting a wide range of concerts and other events right across the arts, including readings, literary events and workshops. In 1988, the National Poetry Library also moved into the Royal Festival Hall, with Seamus Heaney presiding over the opening ceremony.

Over the years, there have been various changes and alterations to the building itself, many of which have been controversial, given the architectural importance of the Royal Festival Hall and its continuing role in the cultural life of the capital. During the mid-Sixties, the LCC's design team was asked to address the problems created by the limited provision of service spaces and offices in the original building. The building was extended to the south, creating more space over five levels for dressing rooms, practice rooms, offices and other much needed ancillary spaces, such as plant rooms, while the rear elevation was redesigned as part of this process. Given this and other additions to the western elevation, the LCC design team – which included Norman Engleback and Robert Maxwell – decided to fully update the exterior façade, including the river frontage, where the changes in fenestration created a more rigorous, rhythmic pattern and arguably increased the sense of connection to the river.

In its listing statement of 1988, English Heritage/Historic England suggested that 'the additions of 1963–64 completed the building by extending circulation and restaurant space at the front and adding offices at the back'.[26] It also suggests that by extending the elevated terraces

RIGHT Recent revisions to the Festival Hall have included the refurbishment, by Conran & Partners, of the riverfront restaurant, now known as Skylon.

around the building during the Sixties, it helped to create a 'conceptual link' with the neighbouring Hayward Gallery (see page 104) and Queen Elizabeth Hall (see page 86) completed by Norman Engleback's team a few years later in 1967–68, despite the radical differences in the aesthetic style of later members of the South Bank grouping.

While there has been much debate over the changes made to the Royal Festival Hall during the Sixties and beyond, particularly concerning circulation routes and the open integrity of the foyers, the character of the building was not radically altered while the warm, Scandinavian-inspired personality of the auditorium was largely respected.

This was also true of the more recent renovation programme led by Allies & Morrison, completed in 2007. The total seating capacity of the auditorium was reduced and careful changes made to improve the acoustics, but the process was sensitively managed, with most original features lovingly retained and restored, including the Robin Day seating and Sadie Speight tapestries, while the organ was also reconfigured and reinstalled. The Allies & Morrison refurbishment also saw welcome improvements to the foyers that helped to create more flexible and fluid communal spaces, while reclaiming lost zones around their edges. There were also a number of more technical updates that help staff accommodate the daunting logistical challenges of staging fast turnaround events and performances. In these ways and others, the Royal Festival Hall has managed to evolve yet still reflects the optimism and intent of the post-war period that helped to shape the invention of this landmark building.

OPPOSITE & ABOVE The interiors of the Skylon restaurant include multiple references to the building's mid-century heritage.

NATIONAL FILM THEATRE

British Film Institute (BFI) Southbank – Norman Engleback, Leslie Martin, Frank West, 1957

INTRODUCTION

The origins of the National Film Theatre building, now known as the British Film Institute (BFI) Southbank, stretch back to the Festival of Britain. Film and television were identified as important themes for the 1951 Festival itself, with the influential and well-established modernist architect Wells Coates invited to design two complementary pavilions to the rear of the South Bank site, sitting side by side on York Road. The two-storey Television pavilion included displays devoted to the early evolution of the British Broadcasting Corporation (BBC), as well as exhibits on outside broadcasting and news coverage. The Telekinema (or 'Telecinema', as it was also known) next door was 'the first cinema in the world to be specially designed and built for the showing of both films and television'.[27]

The excitement of the Telekinema was largely hidden away inside the building itself, which

RIGHT The recently updated front entrance to the BFI Southbank, slotted underneath Waterloo Bridge.

SOUTH BANK
LONDON
Let's be social
LET'S DO
LONDON

NATIONAL FILM

included an auditorium seating 400 people along with sophisticated sound and projection equipment, as well as aerials for receiving BBC broadcasts of key events. But the majority of the Telekinema's programme was devoted to specially commissioned documentaries and 3D films, produced for the Festival of Britain, and curated by the British Film Institute (BFI), which was founded in 1933 initially to promote the development of film and television in Britain and, later, adding the important role of establishing and caring for a national film archive.

After the Festival of Britain, the majority of the temporary pavilions on the South Bank site were cleared and removed, but the BFI managed to hold on to the Telekinema for a few more years, although the location alongside York Road was soon identified as the setting for the development of the Shell Centre and neighbouring buildings, completed during the early Sixties. The BFI needed to find a new home, ideally close by, with the undercroft of Waterloo Bridge suggested by the London County Council (LCC). This became the rather unlikely setting for a new cinema and BFI headquarters known as the National Film Theatre (NFT), completed in the space of just 15 months and opened in 1957. Extended during the Eighties and Nineties and updated again more recently, the cinema plus its bar/restaurant remain a much loved venue today, still hosting major events such as the London Film Festival.

LEFT The original NFT signage on the side of Waterloo Bridge was restored as part of a recent renovation programme.

CONTEXT

The southern undercroft beneath Waterloo Bridge, which was rebuilt in 1945, had already been put to good use during the Festival of Britain. This was the location for the Thames-side Restaurant, also known as the Riverside Restaurant, 'serving meals at popular prices with self-help service'.[28] It was designed by Jane Drew and Maxwell Fry, who – like Coates – were influential figures in the evolution of early modernism in Britain and, later, worked in Africa and India, where they assisted Le Corbusier and Pierre Jeanneret with the epic task of designing the new provincial capital city of Chandigarh.

Drew had been offered a very limited site alongside the riverfront, but realized that she would be able to design something more substantial and capture wider views over the Thames if she pushed her way under the bridge itself:

'I immediately went to [Festival director] Sir Gerald Barry and asked if we could have a little more land. He replied that if I could square things with the Port of London Authority he had no objection. This proved to be quite a job because they wanted the building designed so that it would collapse at once if hit by a ship. The greatest problem, however, was how to erect it, as it was going to be the last part of the site to be built on.'[29]

Drew and Fry opted for a modular approach involving the prefabrication of units that could be easily assembled on site, creating a distinctive pleated aluminium roof canopy that pushed outwards from under the bridge and stretched along the river frontage to either side. They enlisted artists and sculptors such as Ben Nicholson and Barbara Hepworth to provide artworks for the restaurant, which managed to survive for a number of years following the Festival of Britain even as most of the thematic pavilions were cleared away.

When the BFI approached the LCC asking if they could help them find a new home, following the demise of the Telekinema, the architecture department suggested the site of the Thames-side

ABOVE & OPPOSITE The BFI makes the most of its unusual South Bank site, imaginatively working around its position underneath and alongside Waterloo Bridge.

Nelson
SOUTHBANK CENTRE
HAYWARD GALLERY
BFI SOUTHBAN

Restaurant, given that it was always intended to be a temporary structure. The call from the BFI came in 1956, shortly before the then head of the LCC's architecture department, Leslie Martin, left to take up his post as the head of the architecture school at the University of Cambridge. Before he left, Martin entrusted the NFT project to Norman Engleback, who had been part of the LCC team since 1953. Although Engleback officially reported to LCC deputy architect Frank West, he famously enjoyed a good deal of autonomy during Martin's tenure and sought to preserve his independence. He was only in his late twenties by the time the NFT project came up, but had already made his mark with his work on the National Recreation Centre at Crystal Palace, now known as the National Sports Centre, which was completed in 1954. The design of the NFT is largely credited to Engleback, who took charge of the project and set it in motion, working to a tight deadline to ensure that the new building would be ready in time for the BFI's move from the Telekinema in 1957.

ABOVE & OPPOSITE The unique character of the BFI Southbank and its role as a working, welcoming cinema have been enhanced during the recent renovations of the building.

NFT1 & 2

BOX OFF

E & CINEMAS
DIGITISED AND PRESERVED
FOR YOU

DESIGN

Like Drew and Fry before him, Engleback found himself pushing his way under Waterloo Bridge, assisted by a young design team mainly consisting of recent graduates. Yet the BFI brief included a request for a 500-seat auditorium, along with service areas and administrative spaces, so Engleback began exploring how far back into Waterloo Bridge's southern vault he could go.

'This vault was sealed by an opening that contained part of the original [John] Rennie bridge with Doric columns and a balustrade,' said Engleback. 'You can imagine that the historic buildings associations were up in arms… but they were overruled and the columns were taken down and converted into ashtrays, but the balustrade was taken down and carefully stored.'[30]

The proposed designs were first published during the summer of 1956. They saw Engleback pushing the main auditorium as far under the bridge as possible, with the screen positioned at almost the furthest point and the auditorium then splaying outwards in a wedge-shaped plan populated by curving, concentric lines of seating. The shape of the auditorium allowed for modest spaces to either side of it, including a conference room, while more public areas were arranged around the entrance and foyer facing the river. A modest upper level, again towards the river frontage, contained the projection room as well as a small secondary theatre, 'intended for editing and compiling programmes by the institute without the use of the large auditorium'.[31]

The greatest challenge was undoubtedly fitting the auditorium under the recesses of the bridge vault, which involved gently excavating downwards while designing a bespoke, internal roofing system that would create an acoustically sound and secure environment for screenings.

'The roof was a series of triangles suspended from the roof [of the bridge],' said Engleback. 'The bridge moves and there are a couple of

ABOVE & OPPOSITE The principal BFI Southbank auditorium, known as NFT1, remains an enticing and glamorous venue.

damper columns but we were told by the engineers that if we moved the damper columns the bridge would collapse. But we had to move them to one side to make more space for the auditorium, so for a period of four weeks it didn't have any columns and nothing happened. It had to be done.'[32]

The building opened the following autumn, much as planned. Engleback managed to squeeze in plant rooms behind the auditorium screen, as well as placing other amenities, stores and offices within compact spaces that made use of every available square foot, much like the design of a ship's interior. The specifications were worked out in conjunction with the BFI, including the need for a flexible screening system capable of coping with a range of film formats and with a degree of inbuilt future proofing. As *Architects' Journal* magazine noted in its coverage, the bridge itself formed an extended canopy that protected the entrance to the NFT: 'This means that the bridge will act as a shelter during bad weather but also that audiences will be conditioned to the dark auditorium by the relatively dark area under the bridge.'[33]

OPPOSITE & ABOVE As well as the cinemas at BFI Southbank, the complex also includes the Reuben Library, which holds one of the world's largest collections of books and journals related to film and the moving image.

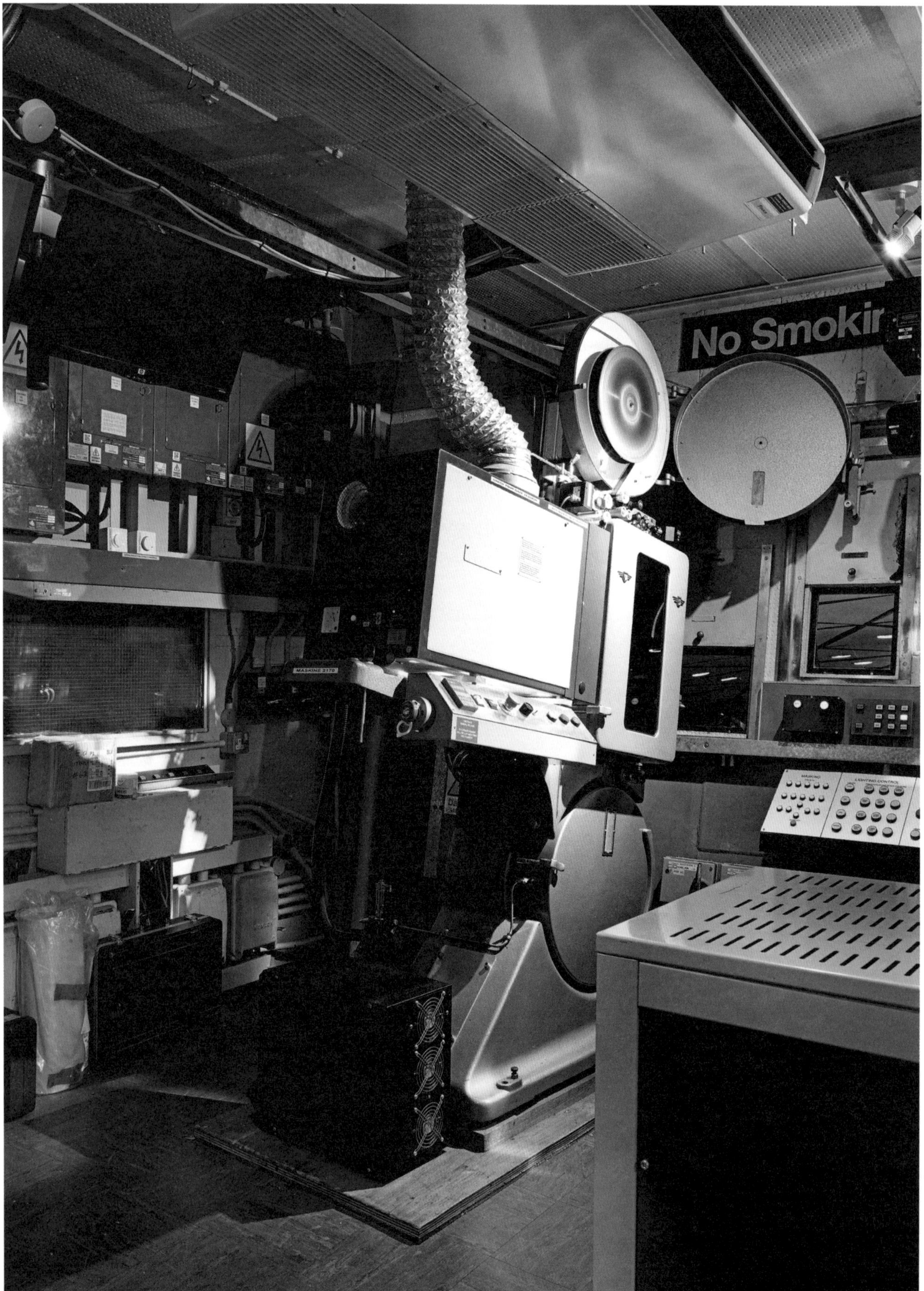
No Smokir

The NFT was opened by Princess Margaret and the Italian actress Gina Lollobrigida on 15 October 1957. That morning, says Engleback, the LCC's new chief architect, Hubert Bennett, visited the building: 'He was very pleased with what he saw,' says Engleback, 'but he had nothing to do with it all.'[34] Deputy architect Frank West kept 'a watching eye' over the drawings, but the NFT marked the first of a series of major new buildings on the South Bank designed by teams headed by Engleback, including the Hayward Gallery (see page 104) and the Queen Elizabeth Hall (see page 86), which helped to realize the LCC's long-term plan of creating a new campus of the arts around the Royal Festival Hall.

OPPOSITE & ABOVE The original planning of the National Film Theatre made use of every available square foot of space, with technical areas such as the NFT1 projecting room tucked under the arches of Waterloo Bridge.

REVISIONS

Rather like its much larger sibling next door, the NFT has managed to adapt and evolve over the years, suggesting the inherent flexibility of the original design. Now known as the BFI Southbank, the building has been updated and restored on a number of occasions since its opening back in 1957. These changes have included the creation of a much larger social space within the hinterland between the auditorium and the riverfront, mostly occupied by a restaurant and bar, which gives further dynamism to the building, while creating a destination attractive not only to film aficionados but others looking to enjoy the riverside setting in a way that is reminiscent of Drew and Fry's long lost Thames-side Restaurant.

During the Sixties and Seventies there were modest changes to the building that saw it extended towards the river frontage, creating more generously scaled social spaces around the entrance to the NFT, as well as the introduction of a second screen known as NFT2. Not long after, structural changes were made to Waterloo Bridge as part of a major new road scheme, which saw the remaining remnants of the southern stone arches of John Rennie's original 19th-century Waterloo Bridge replaced with fresh concrete supports. These alterations created a possibility to further expand the NFT complex by occupying the additional new spaces under the bridge.

Avery Associates Architects began work on a number of inter-related projects for the NFT and the BFI that spanned the Eighties and Nineties. Chief among these was the Museum of the Moving Image, which opened in 1988 and filled most of the available space created alongside the original NFT, including exhibition galleries plus a new cinema space. Avery Associates also worked on the design and delivery of the nearby BFI IMAX Cinema in Waterloo, completed in 1999.

Following the closure of the Museum of the Moving Image, there was a further wave of revisions at the NFT, which became the BFI

RIGHT Later additions alongside and further under Waterloo Bridge, including the Mediatheque, have fully maximized the site's potential.

Cinemas
BFI Mediatheque
BFI Reuben Library
BFI Shop
BFI bar & kitchen

Southbank in 2007. Architects Buchanan Hartley, working in collaboration with David Adjaye Architects, completed the expansion of the complex by adopting spaces and screens that were previously part of the Museum of the Moving Image, effectively doubling the overall space occupied by the BFI in comparison with Norman Engleback's original design.

The most recent revisions to the BFI Southbank, by Carmody Groarke Architects, have helped to establish a much stronger and clearer identity for the building, particularly around the main entrance under Waterloo Bridge. This was a key part of the update programme, along with further improvements to the restaurant and bar spaces alongside the riverfront promenade and significant upgrades to plant and services.

One of the key ambitions of the project was to highlight the clarity of the site as a working cinema complex, while removing some of the ambiguity that had developed over the various phases of expansion and renewal. One of the

ABOVE & OPPOSITE The recent modernization programme by Carmody Groarke has included the full upgrade of the hospitality spaces at the BFI Southbank.

National Theatre
National Theatre
National Theatre
National Theatre

most dramatic additions is the new entrance canopy, which pushes gently outwards either side of the bridge, while featuring a ribbon of pale fibreglass that illuminates in the evenings like a cinema screen. While this lightbox serves as a tempting beacon drawing visitors to the BFI Southbank, the architects have also created an elevated roof terrace that sits just above but is also sheltered by the underside of the arching bridge. In this way, the primary identity of the building as a cinema has been reinforced, yet its secondary purpose as a place of many pleasures has also been enhanced. Norman Engleback would be pleased to note that his original NFT signage on one side of the building has also been lovingly restored as part of the refurbishment project.

OPPOSITE & ABOVE The refurbishment work includes the provision of a new roof terrace slotted under the bridge arch, as well as the remodelled entrance.

QUEEN ELIZABETH HALL & PURCELL ROOM

Norman Engleback,
Hubert Bennett, Frank West,
Ron Herron, Warren Chalk,
Dennis Crompton et al,
1967

INTRODUCTION

During the evolution of the Royal Festival Hall, there was an early plan for a secondary performance space that would offer a smaller and more intimate setting than the main auditorium. Given the many constraints and complexities of the Festival of Britain site, the idea was shelved in 1951 but remained upon a London County Council (LCC) wish list for the South Bank site. It formed part of an ongoing plan to develop a campus of the arts alongside the Thames, with a range of venues of various kinds and different scales.

The plan was slow to develop, with much debate about the choice of new buildings, their

RIGHT The main entrance is at upper ground level, accessible from the elevated terraces that connect to the neighbouring buildings.

SOUTHBANK
CENTRE
Queen Elizabeth Hall
Purcell Room

exact location on the South Bank site and which stakeholders might be involved in running them. Apart from the Royal Festival Hall itself, the only other major addition to the campus during the Fifties was the National Film Theatre (see page 64), designed by an LCC team led by architect Norman Engleback, that was completed in 1957, with the building neatly slotted under the arches of Waterloo Bridge.

Around the same time Hubert Bennett took over from Leslie Martin as the LCC's chief architect, inheriting a system of largely self-contained design studios sitting under the umbrella of the architecture department based at nearby County Hall. Isaac Hayward, the long-serving leader of the LCC who had been in the post since 1947, continued pushing for the development of the South Bank site, particularly during the early Sixties when he realized that the LCC itself was likely to be abolished and replaced. This eventually happened in 1965, when the Greater London Council (GLC) was established and – even though Hayward's deadline had not been met – there was significant progress on the design and development of both new performance spaces and an associated art gallery, which became the Queen Elizabeth Hall, the Purcell Room and the Hayward Gallery (see page 104).

OPPOSITE & ABOVE The terraces and walkways around the building tie it to the Hayward Gallery and the nearby Festival Hall, while also creating an elevated plaza overlooking the river.

CONTEXT

For many years, the LCC and its architecture department held on to the idea that an additional performance space might be grafted on to the rear of the Royal Festival Hall or placed just behind it. There were substantial changes, alterations and extensions to the Festival Hall in 1963–64, but by then there was already a realization that changes to the adjoining road pattern and nearby Belvedere Road, combined with concerns about the potential acoustic impact of the nearby underground line, meant that a fresh site for a secondary hall would have to be found.

By then the Arts Council had also raised the idea of a new art gallery on the South Bank, which Isaac Hayward and the LCC embraced. Norman Engleback was invited to develop ideas for both the performance space and gallery, which would need to be slotted into a space between the Festival Hall and Waterloo Bridge, where the former Shot Tower turned Festival of Britain beacon had once stood. There was agreement that the new additions should not try and compete with the Festival Hall itself in size or scale, leading to the idea of breaking the new performance spaces and the art gallery into separate but complementary structures sitting side by side.

'It was going to be subservient to the Festival Hall, per se,' said Engleback. 'It seemed to me that some sort of intervening but fragmented pattern of structures would have been a more satisfactory answer. There was also… the planner's brief of what they call "great separation" in those days: traffic on the ground level, pedestrians on the first floor deck. That principle has been abandoned everywhere but was almost the mantra of the early Sixties.'[35]

As an aficionado of classical music, an opera buff and amateur musician, Engleback was determined to ensure that he was well prepared for the challenge of designing a new performance venue. He was able to draw on the LCC's own experience with the Festival Hall and the early acoustic adjustments required in the auditorium,

ABOVE The brutalist character of the raw concrete structure contrasts with the use of characterful timber for the floors and acoustic wall panelling, creating a warm and welcoming environment.

yet he also sought out the advice of consultants and experts, including the London-based conductor and violinist Yehudi Menuhin. Engleback went on a fact-finding trip on the Continent, looking at both performance spaces and galleries, as well as pioneering buildings such as the Italian architect-engineer Pier Luigi Nervi's Flaminio Stadium in Rome designed for the 1960 Olympic Games and featuring an expressive, energetic use of reinforced concrete. As well as visiting Italy, Engleback attended concert halls in Germany and Switzerland.

'It was a very exciting time and I loved every moment of it because they used to be my main interests,' said Engleback. 'For instance when we got to La Scala in Milan [Birgit] Nilsson was singing in *Turandot* with Franco Corelli, the sort of thing you'd give your eyes for and we were given a box to see them in. What more could you want?'[36]

Around the same time, Engleback was building up his own design group at the LCC. It was a young team that included many recent graduates, such as Ron Herron, Warren Chalk and Dennis Crompton, who went on to co-found the radical Sixties architecture collective Archigram, as well as teaching at the Architectural Association. Engleback welcomed their input and ideas, while recognizing that times had changed since the design of the Royal Festival Hall, which was emblematic of the International Style, and that a fresh approach was required.

RIGHT The auditorium's acoustics have been carefully calibrated, assisted by architect Norman Engleback's extensive technical research into performance halls.

DESIGN

Eventually, the LCC decided to proceed with two new performance spaces rather than one. There was the multi-purpose venue that became the Queen Elizabeth Hall, with a symmetrical auditorium seating around 1,000 people. But there was also a request for a second, smaller performance space, the Purcell Room, which would hold an audience of around 370 guests for smaller events, as well as hosting rehearsals. Engleback decided to place these two venues alongside one another, within the same building, and adopt a common design language for them both. But there were also other factors that influenced their design and the choice of concrete for a brutalist ensemble, which included the Hayward Gallery next door.

'At the time when the concert hall was designed there was a proposal to build a heliport at Battersea and there was supposed to be a service which ran along the Thames to Battersea and back,' said Engleback. 'They were using a helicopter called the Fairey Rotodyne that... produced an enormous amount of noise, 130 decibels and absolutely frightening. There was a good deal of concern about whether this would disturb the new concert hall and the Hayward. And the answer to that... was that you could only deal with this with mass.'[37]

Acoustics consultant Peter Parkin advised that the buildings would need a minimum of 40cm (15in) concrete walls to protect them against the noise of the helicopters, as well as traffic running over Waterloo Bridge alongside the new buildings. Engleback was also drawn to the idea of using concrete as a 'unifying element' that would tie together not only the performance venues and the nearby art gallery but also the elevated walkways that would connect them together and also lead round to the Festival Hall, while traffic circulation and service spaces were demoted to the resulting undercroft. Herron and Chalk worked on the design of these walkways as well as the junctions between the different buildings, while Engleback paid particular attention to the interiors and the acoustic quality of the spaces within, which were fitted with Helmholtz resonators to improve the sound quality.

There is a striking contrast between the raw, brutalist exteriors of the Queen Elizabeth Hall plus the Purcell Room and the crafted character of the performance spaces within them. Engleback visited a specialist timber importer in east London and secured a supply of Brazilian Coffee Bean wood veneer, which was used to coat the staggered side walls of the two venues, introducing a striking sense of warmth and personality, while also adding to the acoustic quality of the spaces. The stage of the Queen Elizabeth Hall was designed to be as flexible as possible, consisting of around 15 different component parts that could easily be adjusted and reconfigured, allowing for a wide range of permutations and uses.

Between the inside and outside realms sat the main foyer, which formed an important

ABOVE & OPPOSITE Queen Elizabeth Hall was designed to meet the brief for a flexible venue with seating for a thousand people, creating a more intimate alternative to the Royal Festival Hall.

hinterland. As with the Royal Festival Hall and the Royal National Theatre, the foyer at the Queen Elizabeth Hall was an important and theatrical space in its own right, serving a social role as a meeting place and point of interchange. The foyer interiors were designed with a striking Sixties aesthetic, with mushroom-shaped concrete pillars holding the coffered ceiling with their pyramidal lighting installations while sheltering a fluid, open space punctuated with doughnut-shaped seating units.

Engleback and his team produced an original, accomplished and radical design for the Queen Elizabeth Hall and Purcell Room, which managed to address a whole collection of challenges generated by a complex site and setting. There was, therefore, a good deal of frustration when LCC chief architect Hubert Bennett inspected the designs late in the day, after 12 months of design work, and suddenly demanded changes. Bennett put forward his own hurried design proposal that Engleback and his design team fought against. The objections came late in 1960, with the full designs for the new £4m arts complex due to be released to the public in March 1961.

'He told the group that he wanted his scheme to be pursued and I put up what I thought was a reasonable defence of why it shouldn't be and offered my resignation,' Engleback said. 'I said I wouldn't do it, you'll have a resignation instead, and the group followed me and they all submitted their resignations. This put Bennett in a dilemma. He either had to get a team together who could do it in three months... or he had to find a way of persuading us to withdraw our resignations.

'At the time we were deeply in trouble with Bennett, I spoke to Diana Rowntree of *The Guardian*. And she put in a piece, in *The Guardian*, which in effect told Bennett to let the chaps get on with their own work and not interfere... I'd seen her on earlier schemes, on Crystal Palace, on the Film Theatre, and so on. So I thought this was a likely contact, quite a useful diva, to see if I couldn't move Bennett from his arrogance. It did the trick.' [38]

ABOVE & OPPOSITE A recent restoration programme by Feilden Clegg Bradley has seen the Sixties character of the main foyer restored and enhanced.

Queen Elizabeth Hall
Seats 21–39

REVISIONS

While Bennett and his deputy, Frank West, managed to secure a number of minor alterations and adjustments to the original designs produced by Norman Engleback and his team, the plans were approved unopposed during the early Sixties. Construction and delivery were protracted, however, with the Queen Elizabeth Hall eventually opening in 1967 with an inaugural concert conducted by Benjamin Britten. Just a few months later Pink Floyd played at the Queen Elizabeth Hall, demonstrating in their own unique way the dexterity of the venue. Norman Engleback expressed his delight with the acoustic quality of the two performance spaces, but was disappointed by some of the critical reactions to the uncompromising brutalism of the exteriors, as well as saddened by a number of later alterations.

Like Denys Lasdun's National Theatre nearby, the Queen Elizabeth Hall, the Purcell Room and the Hayward Gallery have remained controversial and exposed to the shifting patterns of architectural taste. Curiously, although many of the neighbouring structures are now listed, Engleback's buildings have not been afforded the protection that listing usually brings. Yet the recent renovation programme by Feilden Clegg Bradley Studios has been highly respectful and successful in carrying the spaces into the 21st century.

In 2012, they were the only architectural practice out of a shortlist of six to suggest 'retaining and refurbishing the existing buildings, while also building around, between and over them' rather than arguing for replacement. 'Our starting point was to restore and renovate the concrete layers of the existing building and to add new spaces where the context allowed,' wrote architect Peter Clegg. 'We felt we should treat the complex as a listed structure even though it had been given a five-year immunity from listing. We had, however, no compunction about adding newbuilt form to the low lying concrete topography which would form a

LEFT The foyer of the Queen Elizabeth Hall offers a communal space full of light and character, orientated towards the terraces and the river.

counterpoint to the existing buildings.'[39]

While a suggestion to reclaim the undercroft of the Queen Elizabeth Hall from the skateboarding community was ultimately rejected, the practice worked on a restoration programme that included major upgrades to services and amenities, as well as decluttering some of the 'accretions' that had compromised both the main performance space and the foyers over five decades. Particular attention has been paid to the materials and detailing, with the ambition of celebrating the craftsmanship of both the board-marked concrete and the timber panelling of the interiors of the auditorium. Many original features, such as the auditorium seating, were carefully retained and preserved within a restoration process comparable to the recent restoration of the Royal Festival Hall next door.

'The public has taken longer to develop a sense of appreciation for the architecture, but it is emerging,' says Clegg. 'We regard it as one of the most experimental buildings of an era known for experimentation. One can understand that in comparison with its Grade II* listed neighbour the National Theatre, it is a building that appears almost adolescent in the development of civic concrete architecture of the late 20th century. But the Hayward Gallery and Queen Elizabeth Hall are arguably more exciting because they are more rebellious and less classically perfect. It is this edginess that has been most challenging for us to work with. For us to work to retain the sense of a building that is all about change, that has an anarchic sensibility at its heart, and that is designed as a facilitator of disruption. Change is the only constant: the great thing about the Southbank is that it will never be truly completed.'[40]

RIGHT The Queen Elizabeth Hall and the Purcell Room sit right alongside the Hayward Gallery, sharing the same architectural team and their intention to create a radical, experimental brutalist design solution to meet the challenge of realizing a cultural campus on the South Bank; the artwork is *You, Me and the Journey* by Souad Abdelrassoul (2022).

ETH HALL
SOUTHBANK

HAYWARD GALLERY

Norman Engleback, Hubert Bennett, Frank West, Ron Herron, Warren Chalk, Dennis Crompton et al, 1968

INTRODUCTION

Upon its completion in 1968, the Hayward Gallery added a completely new element to the South Bank's cultural campus. There was a fine art component to the 1951 Festival of Britain itself, exemplified on the South Bank site by various contributions and on-site installations from artists and sculptors such as Ben Nicholson, Henry Moore, Lynn Chadwick, Barbara Hepworth, John Piper and others. But with just a few exceptions, these were mostly removed from the South Bank site, along with the thematic pavilions, after the end of the Festival itself.

As the South Bank evolved in the years after the Festival, the focus was largely on refining the performance spaces at the Royal Festival Hall and developing the idea of complementary venues, as well as finding a new home for the British Film Institute in the form of the National Film Theatre (see page 64). But the idea of a new art gallery on the South Bank remained on the London County Council's (LCC) agenda and was actively promoted by the council's leader, Isaac Hayward, during the Fifties and Sixties. Hayward's ambitions for a new and bespoke gallery were supported by the Arts

RIGHT The distinctive roofline of the Hayward Gallery, including its restored pyramid skylights, with the London Eye in the background.

HAYWARD GALLERY

Council, who were looking for a new base to host travelling exhibitions.

The Arts Council lent support and advice, while offering to run the gallery initially. The early development funding largely came from the LCC, whose architecture department also led the design and build programme for what eventually became known as the Hayward Gallery. The LCC's chief architect, Hubert Bennett, and his deputy, Frank West, were in charge of the department but the project itself was led by Norman Engleback and his team, who were working concurrently on the designs for the Queen Elizabeth Hall and the Purcell Room (see page 86), situated alongside the Hayward and Waterloo Bridge.

The Hayward shared the same brutalist aesthetic as the Queen Elizabeth Hall next door, with elevated walkways connecting the venues at upper ground level, yet the remits of the neighbouring buildings were radically different, requiring a fully tailored approach to each of them. Just as Engleback embraced a research process and fact-finding mission looking at concert halls on the Continent, which influenced the design of the Queen Elizabeth Hall and Purcell Room, the architect and his team also studied galleries at home and abroad while consulting with the Arts Council, particularly one of its artistic directors, Gabriel White.

LEFT The architecture of the Hayward Gallery adopts a similar brutalist aesthetic to the neighbouring Queen Elizabeth Hall and Purcell Room.

DESIGN

One of the arts venues visited by Engleback was the Wallraf-Richartz Museum in Cologne, where he was impressed by the use of courtyard spaces to display larger sculptures outside. For the Hayward Gallery, he was drawn to the idea of including not only carefully controlled internal exhibition spaces, but also projecting balconies and terraces on top of the gallery and around it, which could be used as sculpture courts.

'The gallery really grew out of the prospect of providing a flexible space of up to 20,000 square feet [1,850 sq m], meeting Gabriel White's demands for exhibitions of all kinds and types with anything from miniatures to frescoes, to probably providing up to two or three simultaneous exhibitions and simple means of access to each, and for outside short courts,' said Engleback. 'And the secret, I thought, for this, was to provide a centralized core of access, so that the lifts would go directly from the workshops up to the various galleries, with the workshops being the places below the public levels and above the car park... and from then on you use the staircase and the lifts.

'The other anxiety I had was that we needed some sort of volumetric difference, exciting changes in space and scale. So you will know that when you go in and look to your left there's a huge ceiling and there's a ramp, which takes you up to a sort of narrow area and then you look down on to another area, and then you go up to the second floor... This seemed to be very satisfactory.'[41]

One of the most contentious subjects was that of light. Engleback was concerned about the impact of natural light on the artworks and exhibits, particularly in terms of conservation, and initially opted for a tightly controlled environment using artificial light within five complementary gallery spaces arranged over two levels. But when Engleback presented his proposals to an Arts Council committee, objections were raised by one of its most eminent members, artist and sculptor Henry Moore.

RIGHT & OPPOSITE The main entrance to the Hayward, which has recently been updated, also sits at upper ground level, accessed via elevated walkways.

HAYWARD GALLERY

'And he, in the nicest possible way, took the strongest exception to cutting out a naturally lit gallery,' said Engleback. 'When I explained that we have open courtyards, which provide him with exactly what he wanted, he said, well, that's not always entirely convenient if it's raining and I think that I'd like to see some sky-lit galleries. And he pressed his point, firmly but gently. I think hyperbole has taken over and we've heard some versions of that in which he thumps the table. But, of course, he didn't do that. He was a very polite man.'[42]

From John Soane's Dulwich Picture Gallery onwards, top-lit exhibition spaces had become an established architectural convention, providing natural illumination while protecting the artworks beneath from the impact of direct sunlight. But for Engleback and his design team, the insistence upon top-lit galleries required significant revisions to his plans for the Hayward, which eventually led to one of its most delightful and distinctive elements.

ABOVE & OPPOSITE The raw concrete interiors of the Hayward Gallery echo the brutalist exteriors, with the spiral staircase recalling the external stairways that connect the upper and lower ground levels of the site.

Working closely with Dennis Crompton, in particular, Engleback began developing a system of glazed pyramids that could be fixed to the roof of the Hayward, which they began testing at a pavilion at Crystal Palace Park, where Engleback had designed the National Sports Centre. To control the sunlight emanating from these skylights, the design team initially experimented with mirrors and then a sub-ceiling made up of translucent Perspex that would sit beneath the pyramids and help control the light levels within the gallery spaces below. They also installed an additional layer of automated blinds that could be used to further control the amount of sunlight spilling into the upper galleries, meeting the requirement for a carefully controlled environment for the display of art while also satisfying Henry Moore's insistence on a top-lit space.

LEFT The freshly restored pyramid rooflights on the uppermost level of the Hayward offer an uplifting, top-lit exhibition space.

DELIVERY

Higgs & Hill were entrusted with the construction of both the Hayward and the adjoining Queen Elizabeth Hall plus Purcell Room, while Ove Arup & Partners were the structural engineers. Construction work began in the summer of 1963, but the many challenges offered by the constrained site, plus the complexity of the designs, meant that the project continued through to 1967, when the Queen Elizabeth Hall opened, with the Hayward Gallery following on in July 1968.

The project required the commitment of a highly skilled team, numbering around 250 at the peak of the project, working with a combination of pre-cast concrete elements and board-marked concrete poured in situ. Both the performance spaces and the Hayward involved the creation of technically demanding and sophisticated spaces, as well as services, while the main elements of the buildings effectively float over the ground plane with walkways and bridges connecting them at first-floor level, where the main entrances are located.

The use of concrete mushroom columns to support parts of the buildings and the walkways was challenging in itself, yet there were also many other sculptural elements such as spiral staircases that also needed to be constructed using cast concrete. The standard of finishing and the quality of detailing remained remarkably high throughout. While the opinions of the architectural critics were mixed, depending on their perceptions of brutalist architecture, structurally the complex was regarded as a work of great originality and ingenuity.

'The adoption of the principle of functional fragmentation of the complex resulted in an exciting array of forms and shapes,' said Ove Arup associate A.J.J. Bartak writing in the *Arup Journal*. 'At the same time, their realization became a predominantly engineering problem and presented the structural engineer with a formidable but at the same time exciting and challenging brief. There was nothing that was conventional or repetitive, nothing that could be

RIGHT An art installation by Agnes Dean, entitled *The Living Pyramid* (2023), can be seen through the open doorway to one of the uppermost exhibition spaces.

solved by the rule book. It demanded a fresh and imaginative approach in the choice and use of materials, and in the creation and application of new construction techniques.'[43]

From the opening of the Hayward Gallery in 1968 – with a retrospective devoted to Henri Matisse – up to 1986, the Arts Council took responsibility for its management and programming, staging exhibitions on both contemporary and period art. It also organized surveys from its own collection of 20th-century British art and sculpture, which consists of thousands of pieces of work gathered from 1946 onwards. A significant proportion of the Arts Council Collection remained at the Hayward after the gallery itself became part of the Southbank Centre and moved under its direct control.

Current Hayward Gallery director Ralph Rugoff argues that the 'democratic' and 'idiosyncratic' character of the building's architecture has served as a catalyst for artists, who 'have embraced and celebrated the gallery's

RIGHT Cristina Iglesias' *Pabellón de Cristal* (2014) exhibited during the Hayward's *Dear Earth: Art & Hope in a Time of Crisis* exhibition.

unique features to create truly memorable experiences of how art and architecture can work together'. More than this, Rugoff suggests that the Hayward 'pioneered a new conception of the museum and gallery as a civic space':

'It did so by emphasizing the importance of its outside areas, as well as creating features that connected inside and outside (even as the gallery simultaneously embodied some distinctively bunker-like qualities). Rather than a hermetically sealed citadel or sanctuary from the world around it, the Hayward suggested a model of the gallery as a partially porous forum – a kind of urban oasis where you could look at the city, and other people, as well as art. The Hayward really started all that.'[44]

ABOVE & OPPOSITE The concrete stairs and other integrated architectural elements have the look of giant sculptures within the context of the exhibition spaces.
OVERLEAF An installation by Himali Singh Soin, entitled *we are opposite like that* (2017-2022).

Exhibition
continues

REVISIONS

As with the other venues and institutions on the South Bank, the Hayward Gallery has seen a number of changes and alterations over the decades. In 2003 architects Haworth Tompkins, who have also worked extensively at the National Theatre (see page 124), created a new entrance pavilion to help improve access to the Hayward, while collaborating with artist Dan Graham on the design of an elliptical roof pavilion. These changes added to the provision of social and educational spaces at the gallery, which were previously quite limited.

More recently, architects Feilden Clegg Bradley completed an extensive refurbishment and upgrade programme at the Hayward, as well as the Queen Elizabeth Hall and Purcell Room. The practice's approach to the gallery, as well as its neighbours, was respectful throughout, aiming to 'work with the strengths and opportunities' while resolving any 'dysfunctionality and decay'. One of the key ambitions for the Hayward was to restore the pyramid skylights and revive the natural lighting system, which had failed many years earlier. While maintaining their original outline form, the steel-framed pyramids were carefully redesigned using opaque white glass on their south-east and south-west faces to limit direct sunlight but using clear glass on the other faces, which now allow glimpses of the sky above from the upper galleries. The thermal envelope of the roof was improved and a full metre of ceiling height regained internally, adding to the sense of space, volume and light.

Such improvements and subtle upgrades have brought the Hayward Gallery into the 21st century. At the same time, there is a growing acceptance of the brutalist beauty of the building itself, and its neighbours, just as Norman Engleback hoped for back in the Sixties.

'I think the Hayward and the Queen Elizabeth Hall were very much of their time,' said Engleback in 2001. 'There has been a lack of sympathy about the South Bank, which I think is rather sad, because I still think those buildings are very good buildings... They are regarded as a work of the Sixties, the concrete era, but it will come again I think and people will begin to take some account for it. I know that younger people really enjoy it and our artists enjoy the building. I have never been back without being excited... but then I suppose that's bias, isn't it?'[45]

OPPOSITE & ABOVE The revitalized Hayward Gallery continues to form a unique part of the cultural life of the South Bank; the sculpture reflected in the window is by Jenny Kendler.

NATIONAL THEATRE

Denys Lasdun & Partners,
1976

INTRODUCTION

It is just a short walk along the riverside promenade from the Royal Festival Hall to the National Theatre. The two South Bank landmarks have much in common, offering performance stages of international importance, while also seeking to provide democratic spaces that include welcoming foyers and communal zones, which enrich life along the waterfront. In various ways, the two buildings explore themes of modern monumentality while establishing positive connections with their surroundings and tying themselves to the Thames.

Yet, in other ways, the Festival Hall (see page 38) and the National Theatre offer dramatic contrasts. They represent a journey through 20th-century modernist architecture, from the International Style aesthetic of the former, completed in 1951, to the uncompromising late brutalism of the latter, completed in 1976. Between the two stand other key markers within the evolution of post-war British architecture, such as the Queen Elizabeth Hall (see page 86) and the Hayward Gallery (see page 104).

The National Theatre marked the culmination of the long-held ambition of developing a cultural campus on the South Bank, encompassing a variety of venues that would, in turn, accommodate a range of typologies within the world of the arts. There is no doubting the

RIGHT The National Theatre has become, over time, an iconic presence in terms of its architecture and its own creative output.

National Theatre
National Theatre
National Theatre

National Theatre

sophistication and originality of Denys Lasdun's temple on the Thames, yet it was also the most controversial architectural statement situated on the South Bank, generating a spectrum of very different responses.

For Lasdun's supporters it was his masterpiece, exploring to the full his ideas about stratified architectural forms and the way architecture relates to the surrounding landscape, with the riverside setting allowing him a golden opportunity to take his thinking to a new level and enabling his dynamic building to breathe. For others, the National was extreme in its unadorned materiality and its raw, sculptural, brutalist aesthetic.

'It is a serious building, the product of a movement which is basically serious, not to say puritanical,' said the critic Mark Girouard just after the National Theatre had opened. 'Because of this it is unlikely, as a landmark, to inspire immediate affection; it is a smoulderer, not a fizzer.'[46]

Over time, Lasdun's masterwork has smouldered successfully. Slowly but surely, it has seduced audiences of all kinds with the technical brilliance of its three performance spaces and the dramatic volumes of its foyer, which Lasdun always regarded as the National's fourth stage. Despite being at the centre of often heated debates about architectural taste during the Eighties and Nineties, the National Theatre is now treated with much affection and admiration by generations who have grown up with the building and have been won over by its unique character. For some, acceptance may have taken half a century, but the National Theatre feels as though it truly belongs upon the South Bank.

LEFT The unique form and structure of the National Theatre fully explores Lasdun's ideas about stratified, or layered, buildings and their relationship to the landscape.

CONTEXT

The idea of creating a British national theatre stretches as far back as the late 19th century and was proposed periodically during the first half of the 20th century. Abercrombie and Forshaw's *County of London Plan* of 1943 for the London County Council (LCC) raised the prospect of creating a major new theatre on the South Bank as a key ingredient of a new cultural complex, with both the LCC and central government supporting the idea of creating a national theatre here by the late Forties and the time of the Festival of Britain.

Following the 1951 Festival, part of the former South Bank Exhibition site between County Hall and Hungerford Bridge was proposed as a suitable location for the project by the LCC. The dialogue between the government and the LCC continued over many years, with discussions about budgets and funding, but eventually Laurence Olivier was appointed to serve as the

ABOVE & OPPOSITE The terraces, verandas and outdoor spaces around the National Theatre are an important part of the overall composition, forming a hinterland between the building itself and the riverside frontage.

National Theatre

first artistic director of the National Theatre in 1962, based at the Old Vic Theatre in Waterloo, and at the Old Vic Theatre Annexe on The Cut, designed by architects Lyons Israel Ellis (1958) and later known as the Royal National Theatre Studio. Olivier staged many landmark productions with the National Theatre Company at the Old Vic, beginning with *Hamlet* in 1963, starring Peter O'Toole. That same year, the National Theatre Board was established and the job of selecting an architect for a bespoke building on the South Bank finally began.

A National Theatre building committee was formed, which included Olivier and John Gielgud among its members. The committee opted for a limited architectural competition, organized by the Royal Institute of British Architects, which produced a shortlist of 20 potential practices. These included major British architects such as Frederick Gibberd, who designed Liverpool Metropolitan Cathedral (1967), as well as international names such as Philip Johnson.

OPPOSITE & ABOVE The raw brutalist character of the building has been softened by landscaping over the years, without disturbing its intrinsic personality.

'The thing was most of the architects came in groups with their partners... but Denys Lasdun arrived entirely alone,' said Olivier. 'Very theatrical. He just sat there: bright, confident and competent to answer all the questions himself... That was immensely effective and of course, as he knew perfectly well, quite touching. We didn't want anyone who had designed a theatre before, we wanted to find a new soul. During the interview Lasdun put his finger on it, very cleverly. He said that surely the most important aspect of what we are talking about is the spiritual one. Oh, my dear! We all fell for that. Well, he was a unanimous choice, we knew we'd got by far the most suitable man and probably the most brilliant man in England.'[47]

Lasdun and his partners began working on the scheme soon after being appointed in 1963, developing ideas over the next few years for the site adjacent to County Hall. At this point, the brief encompassed both the National Theatre and Opera House, sitting side by side on the riverbank, although potentially overshadowed by the mass of the Shell Centre's (1962) high-rise towering just behind them, while the Festival Hall would be right next door, separated only by the Hungerford Bridge. Models and presentations of this early scheme from 1965 offer buildings that have certain familiar elements in common with what was eventually to become the National Theatre, particularly the use of tiered terraces facing the river, yet the idea of two, similar sibling buildings placed together gave additional resonance to these original proposals.

In 1966, however, Harold Wilson's Labour government decided that the Opera House was unaffordable and that the project should focus on the National Theatre alone. The Greater London Council (GLC), which had just replaced the LCC, offered a fresh but smaller site alongside Waterloo Bridge, within an area known as Prince's Meadow. At that time, Norman Engleback and his team were already working on the construction of Queen Elizabeth Hall and the Hayward Gallery just on the other side of Waterloo Bridge, while the National Film Theatre sat between the Lasdun and Engleback sites, slotted underneath the bridge itself.

ABOVE & OPPOSITE The multiple layers of board-marked concrete enhance the stratified form of the building, while the vertical towers provide a foil for the powerful horizontals of the ziggurats.

DESIGN

While Lasdun was able to carry over some ideas from his earlier scheme, the fresh setting naturally required a new design, which responded not only to the river but also to the new position alongside Waterloo Bridge. Consulting with the building committee, Lasdun settled on the solution of three theatrical spaces sitting within a single building, while the main foyer, communal areas and terraces looked out over the Thames and the riverside walk. As with the earlier scheme, the building was staggered as it faces the river, with the terraced ziggurats ascending towards the concrete bulk of the central fly tower.

The Olivier Theatre, sometimes compared to a Greek amphitheatre, features an open stage and two tiers of semi-circular seating at stalls and circle levels, seating around 1,150 people, arranged at right angles to the axis of the performance area. A spacious stage area combined with the soaring fly tower above was intended to create a versatile theatrical setting suited to a wide range of productions, supported by an extensive and carefully conceived backstage realm, which is a complex world in its own right, pushing back upon the site towards Upper Ground.

The Lyttelton Theatre is a more conventional theatre space, seating around 900 people, with seating directly facing the proscenium stage in two tiers. The third theatre was originally known as the Cottesloe, but is now known as the

ABOVE & OPPOSITE Lasdun thought of the foyers and communal spaces at the National Theatre as the fourth stage, serving a vital role in terms of offering both a warm welcome and social pleasures.

The
Lyttelton
Theatre

Dorfman Theatre, originally holding an audience of 330 but more recently upgraded to just over 460 with a range of possible configurations for the seating.

The public areas in and around the three theatres were just as important to Lasdun as the performance spaces themselves. They offer an extraordinary journey through the building, with its various shifts and changes in volume and scale, as well as carrying visitors across multiple levels. Lasdun provides generous contemplative spaces, where it is possible to spend time appreciating the beauty of the many layers of board-marked concrete, the sculpted stairways and the coffered ceilings. But there are also many more intimate zones within the National Theatre, such as the principal restaurant, now known as the 'Lasdun', situated between the ground floor and level one.

The multi-layered terraces and balconies form an important hinterland of halfway spaces between the interior world of the National and the riverfront. They also provide various points of connection with the Southbank Centre alongside, tying in with the walkways leading towards the Hayward, Queen Elizabeth Hall and the Royal Festival Hall.

'The architecture is, as it were, almost without façades but with layers of building like geological strata,' said Lasdun of the National Theatre, 'connected in such a way that they flow into the surrounding riverscape and city. The building really is an extension of the theatre into the everyday world from which it springs.

'Strata are important to me and they allow the building to extend itself… Above all, they provide rich sockets which mediate between the outside of the building and the inside and, for me, they satisfy formal requirements in the sense that they unify a programme of building and give it scale. And, in a sense, they also satisfy symbolic requirements, in that they give visual expression to the essential public nature of the building, where human contact is enriched and a common experience can be shared.'[48]

Given the complexity of the National Theatre, it is not surprising perhaps that it took so long to perfect the designs and begin construction, with

ABOVE & OPPOSITE With three separate performance theatres and a multitude of backstage spaces, the National is a highly complex building tied together by circulation routes, each with a specific character of its own.

work finally getting underway on site in 1970 and the topping-out ceremony taking place in 1973. As well as the many technical and structural challenges of building the three theatres themselves, as well as the foyers and spaces around them, the substantial backstage facilities include set storage areas, workshops, costume studios and service spaces, as well as rehearsal rooms and dressing rooms, which are arranged around an internal courtyard. When the public areas, the theatres and the backstage zones are all added together, the scale of the National is that of a self-contained village in its own right.

By 1976, when the National Theatre finally opened its doors, Laurence Olivier had been succeeded as artistic director by Peter Hall. But the model of an actor-led company had been firmly established and a reputation for excellence and innovation proven by a series of seminal National Theatre productions, running from 1963 onwards. Hall was able to carry this model forward – working with the country's greatest writers, actors and directors – while managing the transition from the venue of the Old Vic to Lasdun's new National Theatre, as well as dealing with some of the critical assessments directed at Lasdun's landmark:

'At the National, Lasdun is… working in a style which, because it is monumental outside, is regarded by those who've not been inside as perhaps a little inhuman,' said Hall in 1977. 'But he's succeeded in making it work because the scale is correct: it is human. His foyers depend upon being thronged with people. People immensely enjoy being in the building: they are drawn to the magnificent city views and the exciting spaces. It may to some look too splendid, even formidable from outside. I would say it has grace and proportion. And inside it's marvellously human.'[49]

RIGHT The interiors of the Lyttleton Theatre, one of the three performance spaces within the National, featuring an adjustable proscenium stage.

RESPONSES

The National Theatre was certainly the most important but also the most controversial project of Denys Lasdun's career. Architectural critics and commentators agreed upon the undoubted significance of the building and celebrated its successful realization after so many decades of development. Yet the uncompromising use of unadorned concrete combined with rigid cubist forms was divisive even among titles such as *The Architectural Review*, *The Architects' Journal* and *Architectural Design*, which had long respected Lasdun's work.

'In architectural terms the theatre has an undeniable excitement in its sculptural and spatial effects,' said *Architectural Design* magazine, reflecting upon the coverage. 'However, it's the concrete that's hardest to stomach, especially since just over the bridge the Hayward Gallery has in just over ten years succeeded in reducing an artistic showcase to a fair replica of the relics of a wartime bunker.'[50]

There was a feeling by the mid-Seventies, even among many architectural critics and commentators, that the tide had turned against brutalism. Despite devoting an entire special issue to the National, *Architectural Review*'s editor Colin Amery was also guarded in his conclusions, recognizing that the building would inevitably generate mixed reactions:

'Denys Lasdun is a very black and white architect, he does not compromise. His National Theatre is a strong, almost elemental building that glories in the strict geometry of space and in the unrelieved use of raw concrete. From the outside the building appears to be deliberately primitive, a huge lumpen formation that rises from the riverbed like a concrete iceberg. To most eyes the abstract and cubist forms of the exterior are still alien, it is a citadel defending some abstract cult that is known and loved only by a small elite. But once the citadel is entered there is an immediate sense of organized space that is comprehensible and moving. The awesome solidity opens up and the public foyers give a sense of dignity and grandeur which elevates them above the mundane nature of their concrete surfaces. There is in this building a sense of some fundamental occasion, a gathering of people to witness some shared ritual.'[51]

Having spent around ten years working on the National Theatre, Lasdun spent the next 20 years defending it. The creative output of the National under Peter Hall and then Richard Eyre flourished, yet the building itself became emblematic of the style wars that broke out during the Eighties and early Nineties, at a time when post-war architecture and modernism were being widely attacked. During the late Eighties, the then Prince of Wales suggested in his television series and subsequent book, *A Vision of Britain*, that 'the National Theatre seems like a clever way of building a nuclear power station in the middle of London without anyone objecting'. 'I try very hard, I must say,' said the future King Charles III, 'to persuade myself to appreciate this sort of architecture, but I can't'.[52]

The National Theatre was not the only target singled out in *A Vision of Britain*, which 'helped

ABOVE & OPPOSITE The contrasting auditoriums of the Lyttleton (above) and the Olivier Theatre (opposite). The Olivier Theatre is the largest performance space at the National, with seating for 1,100 people.

demonize the modern movement',[53] as Lasdun put it. Yet it drew the architect directly into the increasingly bitter skirmishes of the style wars, played out upon the pages of the newspapers, and inevitably made him more protective of his work and of the National in particular. Although he once said that 'buildings should speak for themselves',[54] the architect increasingly began speaking for them, defending his portfolio with all of his energy as he fought back against the critics and anyone who sought to alter or amend his work, especially the National Theatre, right up until his death in 2001.

Yet it was also true that Lasdun had many supporters and not only within the architectural profession itself. Sometimes these voices of support came from surprising and unexpected quarters, as was the case with the poet and conservationist John Betjeman. During the mid-Seventies, Betjeman wrote a handwritten letter to Lasdun, full of praise for the National:

'Now I was going to write to tell you a momentary exaltation I had. I was in a taxi with Osbert Lancaster last week on my way to the City from County Hall. It was a fine crisp morning, blue sky and little mist about. As we crawled out of that hell hole they have dug in front of Waterloo Bridge, I gasped with delight at the cube of your theatre in the pale blue sky and a glimpse of St Paul's to the south of it. It is a lovely work and so good *outside*, which is what matters most...'[55]

LEFT The rich architectural detailing of the National Theatre includes the extraordinary coffered ceilings and the board-marked staircases; the statue of Laurence Olivier honours the first artistic director of the National, from 1962-1973.

REVISIONS

Denys Lasdun famously resisted any significant changes to the National Theatre during his lifetime. Even though one of the most dramatic additions to the immediate setting was Lasdun's own IBM Building, situated right next door and completed in 1984, the architect argued against alterations to the exteriors of the National and was also suspicious of adjustments to the interiors, publicly questioning updates made during the Nineties.

Yet, like its neighbours along the South Bank, the National Theatre, which was listed in 1994, has also had to evolve and adapt for a new century. In 2007, architects Haworth Tompkins were invited to produce a comprehensive conservation management plan for the 'revitalization' of the National, which became known as the NT Future project, involving extensive research and consultation with the leadership team at the theatre itself, as well as other stakeholders, such as English Heritage/ Historic England, Lambeth Council, the Twentieth Century Society, the Southbank Centre and others. Key ambitions identified during this process included improving public access to the building, updating services and extending the provision of backstage amenity spaces and studios, which had become stretched over the years.

While Haworth Tompkins were clearly respectful of Lasdun's legacy and carefully noted his views, it became clear that significant

ABOVE & OPPOSITE Recent renovations have improved public access to the National, as well as updating the amenities in the communal areas, while also enhancing connections with the riverside surroundings.

alterations were now needed, including adjustments to a number of earlier modifications from the Nineties. Originally, Lasdun had designed the entry sequence with cars in mind and a drop off sequence alongside the riverfront façade, yet this part of the promenade is now pedestrianized, leading to revisions. These changes have established a much closer relationship to Queen's Walk, both around the main entrance foyer and also through a number of reclaimed spaces overlooking the promenade, particularly on the north-eastern corner of the building where a former service yard was converted into a new café and bar, spilling out on to the adjoining terrace.

The former Cottesloe Theatre, now known as the Dorfman, was substantially upgraded and its seating capacity expanded as part of a programme of works to the east of the building, while the Clore Learning Centre was created alongside, enabled by the conversion of former workshop spaces. Addressing the growing pressure upon the backstage realm, Haworth Tompkins created a completely new addition at the rear of the National Theatre known as the Max Rayne Centre, holding fresh workshops, studios and production facilities. The design of this new and bespoke building is deliberately distinct from Lasdun's original composition, distinguished by its own clear architectural identity rather than offering a reinterpretation of the National's brutalist aesthetic.

Other changes within the conservation programme have been subtle, yet also significant in their own way. The signage, for example, has been carefully revived using the original Seventies typefaces as a starting point, while, similarly, the updated lighting schemes within the National have sought to replicate the spirit of Lasdun's original designs but with energy-efficient, sculptural solutions. More generally, introducing bursts of colour and texture within the choice of furniture and furnishings for the interiors has helped to create a more welcoming environment, while still preserving the essential materiality of the concrete walls and extraordinary coffered ceilings. At the same time, landscaping and planting around the

LEFT The National Theatre also features a choice of cafés and restaurants including, appropriately enough, the Lasdun Restaurant.

National has been markedly improved.

'A key quality is the formal geometrical rigour of the plan and section, from the main moves down to formwork setting out and handrail details,' says architect Steve Tompkins. 'With that in mind, we were keen to re-establish the central 45-degree axial symmetry of the main river walk entrance. Lasdun's rigour follows through to his use of materials and so it was crucial for us to respect and restore the clear hierarchy of permanence that he established: the geological bedrock layer of board-marked concrete for the formal front of house areas and principal auditoria and bush-hammered concrete for the workshop plinth; the permanent-but-interchangeable layer of brick infill panels and aluminium curtain walling; and the "flora" of dark Wenge veneers for furniture and fittings along with a unifying carpet on the foyer floors and stairs.

'In his conception, those layers of permanence would be complemented by the play of natural and artificial light and the dynamic tidal flows of "fauna" – visitors, audiences and performances – throughout the day and evening, which Lasdun conceived as an essential, ever-changing element of the architecture. We tried to carry out our changes within the more mutable layers and certainly to leave the concrete sacrosanct.'[56]

Arguably, such changes have not only helped to revitalize the National Theatre but have made it more inviting and, in doing so, have enhanced positive perceptions of the building among a broad audience that stretches well beyond existing admirers of the building and brutalist architecture more generally. Such thoughtful evolution and adaptation is very much in keeping with similar programmes across the South Bank cultural complex.

While Lasdun disliked change where his own buildings were concerned, and sought to protect them from anything that he suspected might interfere with the original ideas behind them, during the later years of his life he could see that the tides of architectural taste were turning again. Just before the turn of the century it was becoming clear that, at last, the shift was in his favour.

RIGHT The journey, or 'promenade architecturale', through the National Theatre surprises and delights, with engaging sight lines and points of connection.

'My information, for what it's worth at this time, is that there is renewed interest in modernism,' said Lasdun in 1996. 'I believe that you have to be unequivocally true to the period in which you seek your living, which is, for me, modern. I do understand that the world has changed and that there are other ways of thinking about it, other forces. And I have become slightly more tolerant in my old age. But not much.'[57]

ABOVE Rich in contrasts and beautifully detailed, the National Theatre is now regarded as one of Denys Lasdun's finest and most accomplished works.

HAYWARD GALL

CHRONOLOGY

1939 – Beginning of World War II
1942 – Beveridge Report on the future of the welfare state in Britain
1943 – Publication of Patrick Abercrombie and John Forshaw's *County of London Plan*, commissioned by the London County Council (LCC)
1943 – First suggestions of a 1951 event to mark the centenary of the Great Exhibition
1944 – Publication of Patrick Abercrombie's *Greater London Plan*, commissioned by the LCC, an extended version of his initial 1943 report
1945 – End of World War II
1945 – Opening of the 'new' Waterloo Bridge designed by Giles Gilbert Scott
1945 – Herbert Morrison, champion of the Festival of Britain, appointed Leader of the House of Commons
1945 – World Trade Union Conference at County Hall on the South Bank
1946 – Robert Matthew becomes the head of the architecture department of the LCC
1947 – First proposals for the Festival of Britain
1948 – Hugh Casson appointed director of architecture for the Festival of Britain's South Bank Exhibition and South Bank site finalized and secured
1948 – Design work begins on the Royal Festival Hall (Bennett, Martin et al)
1948 – National Health Service (NHS) established and National Assistance Act passed, establishing the modern British welfare state
1949 – Construction of the Royal Festival Hall begins
1951 – Festival of Britain
1951 – Opening of the Royal Festival Hall
1951 – Initial opening of the National Film Theatre (NFT) situated at the Telecinema/ Telekinema within the Festival of Britain's South Bank Exhibition site
1952 – Arts Council proposes a new gallery on the South Bank
1952 – End of the wartime Utility Furniture programme
1953 – Leslie Martin becomes the head of the architecture department of the LCC
1953 – Coronation of Queen Elizabeth II
1956 – Hubert Bennett becomes the head of the architecture department of the LCC
1957 – Opening of the National Film Theatre (NFT) in its permanent home under Waterloo Bridge (Norman Engleback et al)
1960–62 – Design of the Hayward Gallery, Queen Elizabeth Hall & Purcell Room (Engleback et al)
1962 – Completion of the Shell Centre (Howard Robertson)
1962 – Demolition of the Shot Tower alongside the Royal Festival Hall
1962 – Maria Callas performs at the Royal Festival Hall
1963 – Denys Lasdun appointed to design the National Theatre & Opera House on the South Bank
1963 – Construction of the Hayward Gallery, Queen Elizabeth Hall & Purcell Room begins
1964 – Royal Festival Hall remodelled, including the rebuilding of the riverside façade, additional spaces to the rear and improved pedestrian walkways
1965 – London County Council becomes the Greater London Council (GLC)
1965 – Denys Lasdun unveils plans for the National Theatre & Opera House
1966 – Plans for an Opera House dropped and the site for the National Theatre relocated further along the river
1967 – Opening of the Queen Elizabeth Hall & Purcell Room
1967 – Design of the National Theatre begins (Lasdun)

1968 – Opening of the Hayward Gallery with exhibitions on the work of Henri Matisse and then Vincent van Gogh
1972 – Completion of the South Bank Television Centre (EPR Architects)
1972 – Completion of King's Reach Tower (R. Seifert & Partners)
1973 – Mike Oldfield performs *Tubular Bells* at the Queen Elizabeth Hall
1973 – Britain joins the EEC
1976 – Opening of the National Theatre
1977 – Completion of Jubilee Gardens on the former site of the Dome of Discovery and neighbouring Festival of Britain pavilions
1978 – Completion of Sea Containers House (R. Seifert & Partners/Warren Platner)
1978–79 – Design of the IBM Building (Lasdun)
1984 – Completion of the IBM Building (Lasdun)
1986 – Abolition of the GLC and partial closure of County Hall; responsibility for the Southbank Centre passes to the Arts Council
1988 – The Southbank Centre Trust is established, taking responsibility for the Centre, and the Royal Festival Hall is listed Grade I by English Heritage
1988 – Terry Farrell appointed to produce a masterplan for the Southbank Centre
1993 – Inaugural Meltdown Festival at the Southbank Centre
1994 – Richard Rogers masterplan for the Southbank Centre
1996 – Completion of the conversion of the Art Deco OXO Tower to mixed use, including shops, restaurants and housing (Lifschutz Davidson)
1997 – Opening of the London Aquarium at the County Hall building, former home of the LCC and GLC
1999 – Rick Mather masterplan for the Southbank Centre
1999 – Walkways directly behind the Royal Festival Hall are removed
1999 – Opening of the IMAX cinema, designed by Avery Associates Architects, in the former 'bull ring' by Waterloo Station
2000 – Opening of the London Eye, aka Millennium Wheel (Marks Barfield)
2000 – Opening of Tate Modern (Herzog & de Meuron) at the former Bankside Power Station
2003 – Hayward Gallery foyer remodelled and extended by Haworth Tompkins Architects and Dan Graham
2007 – Allies & Morrison completes the refurbishment of the Royal Festival Hall
2007 – National Film Theatre (NFT) becomes the British Film Institute (BFI) Southbank
2007 – Haworth Tompkins commissioned to produce a conservation management plan for the National Theatre
2011 – Opening of Queen Elizabeth Hall roof garden
2012 – Redevelopment and reopening of Jubilee Gardens
2014 – Completion of the restoration of the organ at the Royal Festival Hall
2014 – Completion of conversion of Sea Containers House from office use into a hotel known as Sea Containers London (Tom Dixon)
2015 – Restoration, revitalization and extension of the Royal National Theatre by Haworth Tompkins completed
2015 – Publication of a Conservation Plan for the Southbank Centre
2015 – Completion of conversion of King's Reach Tower from office use to residential with the building renamed Southbank Tower (Kohn Pedersen Fox/ Johnson Naylor)
2022 – Redevelopment of the BFI Southbank completed (Carmody Groarke)

FOOTNOTES

1. A phrase attributed to the Festival's director general, Gerald Barry.
2. A second crossing was added for the Festival of Britain itself, while the walkways were eventually replaced in 2002 by the Golden Jubilee Bridges, designed by Lifschutz Davidson Sandilands.
3. Ian Cox, *The South Bank Exhibition*, H.M. Stationery Office, London, 1951, p. 7.
4. A dedicated Commonwealth exhibition was created later, in 1962, within London's Commonwealth Institute, designed by the co-author of the Royal Festival Hall, Robert Matthew, and his colleague Stirrat Johnson-Marshall, with exhibits designed by another former Festival contributor James Gardner; the former Commonwealth Institute building now hosts the Design Museum.
5. Ian Cox, *The South Bank Exhibition*, H.M. Stationery Office, London, 1951, p. 8.
6. Hugh Casson, 'Britain Gets Going Again', *Concrete Quarterly*, Spring 1985, p. 22.
7. Hugh Casson, interviewed by Cathy Courtney, National Life Stories, British Library, 1990–91.
8. Ibid.
9. Hugh Casson, 'Period Piece', in Mary Banham & Bevis Hillier's (eds) *A Tonic to the Nation: The Festival of Britain 1951*, Thames & Hudson, London, 1976, p. 79.
10. Ibid, p. 78.
11. Ian Cox, *The South Bank Exhibition*, H.M. Stationery Office, London, 1951, p. 85.
12. Ibid, p. 31.
13. Brian Edwards, 'Exhibition Design', in Philip Long & Jane Thomas' (eds), *Basil Spence Architect*, National Galleries of Scotland, Edinburgh, 2007, p. 55.
14. Ralph Freeman, 'Festival Structures', in Mary Banham & Bevis Hillier's (eds) *A Tonic to the Nation: The Festival of Britain 1951*, Thames & Hudson, London, 1976, p. 91.
15. Misha Black, 'Architecture, Art and Design in Unison', in Mary Banham & Bevis Hillier's (eds) *A Tonic to the Nation: The Festival of Britain 1951*, Thames & Hudson, London, 1976, p. 79.
16. Architectural Review Editors, *Architectural Review*, Volume 110, Number 656, August 1951, p. 73.
17. Reyner Banham, 'The Style: "Flimsy... Effeminate"?', in Mary Banham & Bevis Hillier's (eds) *A Tonic to the Nation: The Festival of Britain 1951*, Thames & Hudson, London, 1976, p. 198.
18. Interview with the author, April 2016.
19. Ian Cox, *The South Bank Exhibition*, H.M. Stationery Office, London, 1951, p. 88.
20. Ibid.
21. Leslie Martin, unpublished lecture notes for a 1984 Architectural Association seminar, quoted by John McKean in *Royal Festival Hall: Architecture in Detail*, Phaidon, London, 2001, p. 4.
22. Trevor Dannatt, *Modern Architecture in Britain*, Batsford, London, 1959, p. 199.
23. Jean Symons, *Royal Festival Hall: Concert Hall Notebook*, Architectural Association, London, 2000, p. 9.
24. Peter Moro, interview with Louise Brodie, National Life Story Collection: Architects' Lives, British Library, 1996.
25. J.M. Richards, 'The Royal Festival Hall', *Architectural Review*, June 1951, Volume 109, Number 654, p. 355.
26. Historic England list entry 1249756, 29 March 1988.
27. Ian Cox, *The South Bank Exhibition*, H.M. Stationery Office, London, 1951, p. 83.
28. Ibid, p. 91.

29. Jane Drew, 'The Riverside Restaurant', in Mary Banham & Bevis Hillier's (eds), *A Tonic to the Nation: The Festival of Britain 1951*, Thames & Hudson, London, 1976, p. 103.
30. Norman Engleback, interview with Louise Brodie, National Life Story Collection: Architects' Lives, British Library, 2001.
31. 'National Film Theatre, South Bank', *The Builder*, 20 July 1956, p. 92.
32. Norman Engleback, interview with Louise Brodie, National Life Story Collection: Architects' Lives, British Library, 2001.
33. 'LCC's Proposal for a Permanent National Film Theatre', *Architects' Journal*, 19 July 1956, p. 81.
34. Norman Engleback, interview with Louise Brodie, National Life Story Collection: Architects' Lives, British Library, 2001.
35. Ibid.
36. Ibid.
37. Ibid.
38. Ibid.
39. Peter Clegg, 'Respect. Redefine. Renovate' in Jude Kelly et al's *Respecting Brutalism: The Hayward Gallery & Queen Elizabeth Hall at 50*, Feilden Clegg Bradley Studios, London, p. 19.
40. Ibid, p. 22.
41. Norman Engleback, interview with Louise Brodie, National Life Story Collection: Architects' Lives, British Library, 2001.
42. Ibid.
43. A.J.J. Bartak, 'South Bank Arts Centre: Structures', *Arup Journal*, July 1967, p. 24.
44. Ralph Rugoff, Director's Perspective: Hayward Gallery, in Jude Kelly et al, *Respecting Brutalism: The Hayward Gallery & Queen Elizabeth Hall at 50*, Feilden Clegg Bradley Studios, London, 2018, p. 108.
45. Norman Engleback, interview with Louise Brodie, National Life Story Collection: Architects' Lives, British Library, 2001.
46. Mark Girouard, 'Cosmic Connections', in Colin Amery's (ed.), *The National Theatre: An Architectural Review Guide*, Architectural Press, London, 1977, p. 7.
47. 'The Great Experiment: Laurence Olivier Talks to Colin Amery', in Colin Amery (ed.), *The National Theatre: An Architectural Review Guide*, Architectural Press, London, 1977, p. 16.
48. Denys Lasdun, 'Architecture of Urban Landscape', Pidgeon Talks, 1980.
49. 'Breaking the Formal Concept: Peter Hall talks to Colin Amery', in Colin Amery (ed.), *The National Theatre: An Architectural Review Guide*, Architectural Press, London, 1977, p. 45.
50. Architectural Design Editors, 'Grand National', *Architectural Design*, March 1977, p. 224.
51. Colin Amery, 'Conclusions' in Colin Amery (ed.), *The National Theatre: An Architectural Review Guide*, Architectural Press, London, 1977, p. 69.
52. HRH Prince of Wales, *A Vision of Britain*, Doubleday, London, 1989, p. 45.
53. Denys Lasdun, interview with Jill Lever, National Life Story Collection: Architects' Lives, British Library, 1996.
54. Denys Lasdun, *A Language and a Theme: The Architecture of Denys Lasdun & Partners*, RIBA Publications, London, 1977, p. 7.
55. Undated letter from John Betjeman to Denys Lasdun, c. 1973, Lasdun Archive, RIBA Collections, Box LAD/480/10.
56. From an interview with the author; 10 November 2023.
57. Denys Lasdun, interview with Jill Lever, National Life Story Collection: Architects' Lives, British Library, 1996.

DIRECTORY

ALLIES & MORRISON
Founded by Bob Allies and Graham Morrison in 1984, the architectural practice Allies & Morrison worked on a conservation plan for the Royal Festival Hall as well as a major refurbishment completed in 2007. Other conservation projects include a renewal programme for Chamberlin, Powell & Bon's Barbican complex.

AVERY ASSOCIATES ARCHITECTS
Founded by Bryan Avery, the practice designed the Museum of the Moving Image (1988) alongside the National Film Theatre (NFT) on the South Bank, as well as the BFI IMAX Cinema (1999) in nearby Waterloo. Avery Associates Architects also worked on a number of other projects at the NFT during the Eighties.

HOPE BAGENAL (1888–1979)
The architect Hope Bagenal was a specialist consultant in the field of acoustics. As well as working on the refurbishment of the Royal Albert Hall during the post-war period, Bagenal was the chief acoustical consultant for the Royal Festival Hall.

GERALD BARRY (1898–1968)
A journalist and newspaper editor, Gerald Barry was appointed as the director general of the Festival of Britain in 1948. Working in this post until the Festival itself in 1951, Barry was responsible for overseeing the exhibition and selecting the various teams involved, including the appointment of Hugh Casson as director of architecture.

HUBERT BENNETT (1909–2000)
After studying at the Manchester School of Architecture, Hubert Bennett served as Southampton's chief architect followed by a similar post with West Riding's County Council. In 1956, Bennett succeeded Leslie Martin as the head of the London County Council's (LCC) architecture department, continuing in the post after the LCC was superseded by the Greater London Council (GLC). As the head of the department, Bennett oversaw multiple projects – including housing, infrastructure and cultural buildings – as well as multiple teams of architects working within the department, including those responsible for the Hayward Gallery and other additions to the South Bank. Bennett retired from the GLC in 1970 and moved into the private sector.

MISHA BLACK (1910–1977)
The architect, designer and exhibition curator Misha Black was the co-founder of the Design Research Unit, one of the first multi-disciplinary design consultancies of the post-war period. During the Festival of Britain, Black worked under Hugh Casson as a co-ordinator within the architectural team known as the Design

Group alongside Ralph Tubbs, James Holland and James Gardner. Black also directed the exhibition displays at the Dome of Discovery, as well as co-designing the Regatta Restaurant.

BUCHANAN HARTLEY ARCHITECTS
Originally founded in 1987 by Dean Buchanan, who was later joined by partner Matt Hartley, Buchanan Hartley Architects converted the Museum of the Moving Image into additional accommodation and cinema space for the adjoining National Film Theatre. The practice worked in collaboration with David Adjaye Architects on the design of the BFI Mediatheque, which formed part of the project and houses part of the British Film Institute's national archive.

H.T. CADBURY-BROWN (1913–2009)
Architect H.T. Cadbury-Brown trained at the Architectural Association and was appointed by Hugh Casson to design the People of Britain pavilion for the Festival of Britain, as well as the Land of Britain exhibit and the Turntable Café. Later projects included the Royal College of Art's Darwin Building (1963) in Kensington, as well as housing schemes for the GLC.

CARMODY GROARKE
Founded in 2006 by Kevin Carmody and Andy Groarke, Carmody Groarke worked on the RIBA-award winning refurbishment of the BFI Southbank, including a new entrance portico and canopy, completed in 2019. Other projects have included the Windermere Jetty Museum (2019).

HUGH CASSON (1910–1999)
An architect, writer, artist and television presenter, Hugh Casson served as director of architecture for the Festival of Britain from 1948 to 1951, after wartime service with the air ministry. Following the success of the Festival, Casson resumed private practice with colleague Neville Conder, with key commissions including the Elephant & Rhino House (1965) at London Zoo. Casson also established and ran the interior design department at the Royal College of Art while pursuing many other creative pursuits, including designing the interiors for Royal Yacht *Britannia* and illustrating Prince Charles' children's book, *The Old Man of Lochnagar*.

WARREN CHALK (1927–1987)
Having studied painting and architecture at the Manchester School of Art, Warren Chalk joined the architecture department at the LCC, working within Norman Engleback's team on the design of the Queen Elizabeth Hall, Hayward Gallery and other projects. Along with friends, colleagues and fellow team members Ron Herron and Dennis Crompton, Chalk went on to become a member of the Archigram Group during the Sixties.

H.F. CLARK (1902–1971)
Alongside Peter Shepheard (see below), landscape designer and author H.F. Clark worked on landscaping and plant selection for the South Bank Exhibition of 1951, with assistance from Marie Shephard. His books included *The English Landscape Garden* (1948).

WELLS COATES (1895–1958)
Architect and designer Wells Coates' best known projects include the landmark Isokon building (1934) in Belsize Park, London, and Embassy Court (1935) in Brighton. The pioneering modernist was also, along with Maxwell Fry, one of the founders of the influential Modern Architectural Research Group (MARS), known as the British arm of the Congrès International d'Architecture Moderne (CIAM). Wells Coates designed both the Television and Telekinema pavilions for the Festival of Britain.

CONRAN & PARTNERS
As a young designer, Terence Conran presented a number of his textile designs at the South Bank Exhibition. In 2007, the architecture and design practice that Terence Conran founded in 1980, Conran & Partners, completed the refurbishment of the Royal Festival Hall restaurant, which was renamed 'Skylon'.

IAN COX
Ian Cox served as the director of Science & Technology for the South Bank Exhibition of 1951. He was also the author of the official guide book to the Exhibition and played a major part in both establishing and directing its key themes.

DENNIS CROMPTON (1935–)
In 1960 architect Dennis Crompton was invited to join Norman Engleback's team working on designs for the Hayward Gallery and Queen Elizabeth Hall. Along with colleagues Ron Herron and Warren Chalk, Crompton formed part of the Archigram collective and was best known as the group's technician, publisher and archivist. Along with Herron, Crompton was also associated with the Architectural Association for many years.

TREVOR DANNATT (1920–2021)
The British architect and author Trevor Dannatt worked with the LCC architecture department from 1943 onwards and was part of the team working on the Royal Festival Hall under Peter Moro. He also designed 'The Whistle' café at the Power & Production pavilion at the South Bank Exhibition and went on to establish his own practice in 1952.

DAVID ADJAYE ASSOCIATES
As part of the expansion of the former National Film Theatre and its 2007 reinvention as the BFI Southbank, David Adjaye Associates were commissioned to design the BFI Mediatheque

hosting part of the British Film Institute's national archive. The practice has also designed major cultural institutions such as the Smithsonian National Museum of African American History and Culture in Washington DC (2016).

LUCIENNE DAY (1917–2010)
Lucienne Conradi studied at the Croydon School of Art and then the Royal Academy, where she first met her future husband, Robin Day. Her 'Calyx' textiles featured in the Homes & Gardens pavilion of the Festival of Britain, with interiors furniture by Robin, with their contributions helping to generate national recognition for their work. 'Calyx' and other mid-century patterns of the Fifties took inspiration from the natural world, while Lucienne Day's textile designs of the Sixties became increasingly abstract in character with a strong Op Art influence.

ROBIN DAY (1915–2010)
Furniture designer Robin Day studied at the Royal College of Art and began a long relationship with the furniture makers Hille during the late Forties. Many of Day's best known designs were produced by S. Hille & Co., including his famous Polyprop Chair (1963), made with an injection-moulded polypropylene seat and back plus tubular steel legs. Robin Day designed the seating at the Royal Festival Hall, as well as furniture and interiors for the temporary Homes & Gardens pavilion.

RALPH DOWNES (1904–1993)
Organist and organ designer Ralph Downes studied at the Royal College of Music, where he later served as a professor. Downes was commissioned to design the organ for the auditorium of the Royal Festival Hall, positioned just behind the main stage.

JANE DREW (1911–1996)
& MAXWELL FRY (1899–1987)
Husband and wife architects plus practice partners Jane Drew and Maxwell Fry designed the Riverside Restaurant under Waterloo Bridge for the Festival of Britain, asking artist Ben Nicholson to design a mural for the curved entrance to the building, now held by the Tate. Drew and Fry also designed the New Schools pavilion for the South Bank Exhibition. As well as their later projects in Britain, Drew and Fry also worked extensively in Africa and assisted Le Corbusier and Pierre Jeanneret with the development of Chandigarh, the new capital of the Punjab, during the Fifties.

NORMAN ENGLEBACK (1927–2015)
During the Forties, Norman Engleback balanced design work for the London North Eastern Railway (LNER) with his studies in architecture. He went on to work with the Architects Co-Operative Partnership and then joined the architecture department at the LCC in 1952. At a young age, Engleback was promoted to serve as team leader by his then department head, Leslie Martin. Under

Martin's successor, Hubert Bennett, Engleback led the LCC design team working on key South Bank projects such as the Hayward Gallery and Queen Elizabeth Hall.

TERRY FARRELL (1938–)
After working in partnership with Nicholas Grimshaw for 15 years, Terry Farrell established his own practice in 1980. Landmark projects include the iconic MI6 Building (or SIS Building, 1994) and the redevelopment of Charing Cross Railway Station (1990), both situated on the northern bank of the River Thames. During the late Eighties, Farrell was asked to produce a masterplan for the Southbank Centre, which was subsequently superseded by plans from Richard Rogers and Rick Mather.

FEILDEN CLEGG BRADLEY STUDIOS
Originally founded by Richard Feilden and Peter Clegg in 1978, the founding partners were later joined by Keith Bradley to create Feilden Clegg Bradley Studios. The practice now has multiple offices across the UK and won the Stirling Prize in 2008 for its work, in conjunction with Alison Brooks Architects, on the Accordia housing project in Cambridge. In 2018, the practice completed the restoration and updating of the Hayward Gallery, Queen Elizabeth Hall and Purcell Room at the Southbank Centre.

ABRAM GAMES (1914–1996)
During World War II, graphic designer Abram Games served as a war artist and designed wartime information posters. He was appointed to design the official logo for the Festival of Britain, known as the 'Festival Star', featuring a four-pointed starburst topped with the profile of Britannia. As well as featuring on posters and signage, Games' eye-catching and colourful designs also featured in the official 1951 Exhibition catalogues.

JAMES GARDNER (1907–1995)
Following wartime service with the Ministry of Information, exhibition designer, curator and graphic designer James Gardner worked on a number of influential post-war exhibitions, including the 'Britain Can Make It' show of 1946. Gardner was a member of Hugh Casson's Design Group for the South Bank Exhibition of 1951 and designed a number of exhibits, as well as serving as the chief designer of the Battersea Pleasure Gardens, which was the second most visited location of the Festival of Britain. Later projects included contributions to the Brussels World's Fair of 1958 and exhibit design for the Commonwealth Institute (1962).

PETER HALL (1930–2017)
The much respected theatre director Peter Hall was appointed to serve as the artistic director of the National Theatre in 1973, serving in the post until 1988. As well as directing over 30 productions for the National, Hall also oversaw the move from the Old Vic into the bespoke building designed by Denys Lasdun, which opened in 1976.

HAWORTH TOMPKINS
The London-based practice Haworth Tompkins was established in 1991 by architects Graham Haworth and Steve Tompkins. The firm has worked on a number of important projects in and around the South Bank, including updates to the Hayward Gallery and a major revitalization of the National Theatre, completed in 2015, which included a new addition at the rear of the building. In 2008, the practice also completed the refurbishment of the National Theatre Studio on The Cut, Waterloo, designed by Lyons Israel & Ellis during the Fifties and originally known as the Old Vic Theatre Annexe. The practice won the Stirling Prize in 2014 for their work on the Everyman Theatre in Liverpool.

ISAAC HAYWARD (1884–1976)
Labour politician Isaac Hayward was the leader of the LCC from 1947 through to its abolition in 1965, when it was replaced by the GLC. During his tenure, Hayward supported the Festival of Britain's South Bank Exhibition, the development and delivery of the Royal Festival Hall and the evolution of the arts venues that eventually grew up alongside it, many of which were completed after Hayward's departure. The Hayward Gallery was named in his honour.

RON HERRON (1930–1994)
Architect Ron Herron studied at the Regent Street Polytechnic before joining the architecture department at the LCC, working with Norman Engleback on the design of the Hayward Gallery, Queen Elizabeth Hall and other projects. During the early Sixties, Herron and LCC colleagues Warren Chalk and Dennis Crompton became three of the six members of the Archigram collective. Herron was also an influential tutor at the Architectural Association and went on to establish his own practice, Herron Associates, in 1981.

JAMES HOLLAND (1905–1996)
Like his colleague James Gardner (see page 162) at the South Bank Exhibition Design Group, James Holland served at the Ministry of Information during World War II as an artist and graphic designer. He was appointed by Hugh Casson as a key member of the co-ordinating team for the South Bank site, but also worked on other aspects of the Festival, including the interiors of the travelling exhibition ship, *Campania*. Following the Festival of Britain, Holland resumed his career in advertising and was the head of graphic design at Birmingham Polytechnic during the Sixties.

DENYS LASDUN (1914–2001)
Denys Lasdun worked with Berthold Lubetkin's Tecton group during the Thirties after completing his studies at the Architectural Association. Following wartime service with the Royal Engineers, Lasdun established his own practice with innovative projects such as his Keeling House 'cluster block' in Bethnal Green (1955). Key

commissions included the Royal College of Physicians (1964), the University of East Anglia (1968) and the National Theatre (1976), while Lasdun was also the author of the South Bank's IBM Building, situated alongside the National Theatre and completed in 1984.

LIFSCHUTZ DAVIDSON SANDILANDS
Architects Lifschutz Davidson Sandilands designed the two new footbridges across the Thames positioned alongside the Hungerford Railway Bridge, which connects the South Bank to Charing Cross. Known as the Golden Jubilee Bridges, completed in 2002, they replaced earlier versions of the Hungerford walkways. The practice also converted the OXO Tower building further along the South Bank creating a mixture of apartments, shops and restaurants, completed in 1996.

LEONARD MANASSEH (1916–2017)
After completing his studies at the Architectural Association in 1941, Leonard Manasseh served in the Fleet Air Arm during World War II. Following the war, Manasseh worked with Hertfordshire County Council and the Stevenage Development Corporation before winning a competition to design a restaurant for the Festival of Britain, which eventually became the '51 Bar. The project encouraged the architect to found his own practice, Leonard Manasseh & Partners, with later commissions including the masterplan for the National Motor Museum at Beaulieu.

MARKS BARFIELD
Husband and wife architects David Marks (1952–2017) and Julia Barfield (1952–) founded their own practice, Marks Barfield, in 1989. They designed the London Eye, or Millennium Wheel, situated on the South Bank alongside Jubilee Gardens and the former home of Festival of Britain pavilions such as the Dome of Discovery. Other projects include both the Waterloo and Millbank Millennium Piers and the i360 observation tower in Brighton (2016).

LESLIE MARTIN (1908–2000)
Having trained at the Manchester School of Architecture, Leslie Martin became head of Hull University's architectural department in his mid-twenties. In 1948, Martin joined the LCC's architectural unit, serving as deputy architect under Robert Matthew, while also heading the team working on the design of the Royal Festival Hall. Following Matthew's departure in 1953, Martin became the LCC's chief architect, with responsibility for a range of projects including large-scale housing schemes and the ongoing development of the South Bank site. Martin departed the LCC, in 1956, to become the first professor of architecture at the University of Cambridge, continuing his career as an influential educator while also running his own practice, with multiple projects in Cambridge itself, including collaborations with colleague Colin St John Wilson.

RICK MATHER (1937–2013)
The American-born architect Rick Mather established his own practice in London in 1973. His key projects included *The Times* newspaper's headquarters in London Docklands (1991) and the Art & Design Academy at Liverpool John Moores University (2008), as well as multiple new buildings upon the campus of the University of East Anglia (UEA), originally designed by Denys Lasdun. In 1999 Mather completed a new masterplan for the Southbank Centre that replaced earlier versions by Terry Farrell and Richard Rogers. Still in operation, the masterplan included the provision of additional public squares and outdoor spaces, improved connectivity and a focus on pedestrianizing routes around the Centre.

ROBERT MATTHEW (1906–1975)
The Scottish architect Robert Matthew studied at Melville College in Edinburgh and the city's College of Arts. In 1936 he began working as an architect with the Scottish department of health, becoming its chief architect, and then, in 1946, was appointed to serve as LCC's chief architect and planning officer. During his tenure, he oversaw the evolution of the design of the Royal Festival Hall, with his deputy Leslie Martin taking over the department in 1953, when Matthew became professor of architecture at the University of Edinburgh. While continuing his work with the university, Robert Matthew co-founded the practice known as RMJM in 1956 with his colleague Stirrat Johnson-Marshall. During the Sixties, RMJM was much respected for its university campus projects in both England and Scotland, while also designing the Commonwealth Institute in London (1962), now known as the home of London's Design Museum.

ROBERT MAXWELL (1922–2020)
Architect, academic and author Robert Maxwell studied at Liverpool University and began his career working alongside Neville Conder on the design of the Homes & Gardens pavilion for the Festival of Britain. After joining the architecture department at the LCC, Maxwell also worked on alterations to the exteriors of the Royal Festival Hall, finalizing the façade facing the river. Later, Maxwell taught at the Architectural Association and Princeton University.

PETER MORO (1911–1998)
Born in Heidelberg, Germany, Peter Moro studied in Stuttgart, Berlin and Zurich before settling in Britain during the late Thirties. He worked with Berthold Lubetkin's Tecton Group and then, in 1948, became part of the LCC design team working on the Royal Festival Hall, focusing on the interiors of the building. Among many other ingredients, Moro designed many of the textiles within the Festival Hall, including the distinctive, geometric 'Net & Ball' carpets. In 1952, the architect founded Peter Moro & Partners with two colleagues, creating a portfolio focused primarily on housing

but also including campus projects and offices for the Hille furniture group and others (see Robin Day).

HERBERT MORRISON (1888–1965)
Labour Party politician Herbert Morrison was the leader of the LCC during the Thirties and went on to serve in multiple ministerial posts, including Home Secretary within the wartime coalition government led by Winston Churchill, and Leader of the House of Commons in Clement Attlee's post-war administration (1945–1951). During his tenure, Morrison championed the idea and realization of the Festival of Britain, encouraging Attlee's government to sponsor the project in combination with support from the LCC.

LAURENCE OLIVIER (1907–1989)
The actor and director Laurence Olivier was appointed as the first and founding artistic director of the National Theatre in 1962. Originally based at the Old Vic, Olivier established the National Theatre Company and directed many of its early productions, as well as appearing on stage. Olivier was also a member of the building committee that selected Denys Lasdun to design the National Theatre, playing a key part in the evolution of its three performance spaces, including the Olivier Theatre, named in his honour.

BRIAN O'RORKE (1901–1974)
New Zealand-born architect Brian O'Rorke studied at the Architectural Association and the University of Cambridge. He was well known for his design of the interiors of luxurious ocean liners and trains, as well as the design of the Royal Observatory at Herstmonceux in East Sussex (1957). O'Rorke designed both the Natural Scene and Country pavilions for the South Bank Exhibition of 1951.

PHILIP POWELL (1921–2003)
& HIDALGO MOYA (1920–1994)
Having met as students at the Architectural Association, Philip Powell and Hidalgo Moya began working together as Powell & Moya from 1946 onwards. One of the practice's first projects was the Churchill Gardens housing estate in Pimlico, London, which Powell & Moya secured after winning a major design competition, with the development for Westminster Council continuing all the way through to 1962. Yet it was the design of the emblematic Skylon for the Festival of Britain that brought Powell & Moya wider attention, with their futuristic structure realized in collaboration with structural engineer Felix Samuely.

ERNEST RACE (1913–1964)
The British furniture designer Ernest Race was asked to design seating for the Festival of Britain, suited to either indoor or outdoor use. He obliged with two biomorphic chair designs, the Antelope chair and the Springbok chair, made with tubular steel

frames and plywood or sprung seats, both of which could be stacked and were hardwearing. The designs were robust enough to be used upon the terraces surrounding the Festival site.

RICHARD ROGERS (1933–2021)
A founding father of the British high-tech architectural movement, Rogers was much admired for his work on the Pompidou Centre with Renzo Piano (1977), the Lloyd's Register Building (1986) and the Millennium Dome (1999). In 1994, Rogers and his practice produced a masterplan for the South Bank – widely known as 'The Wave' – that envisaged creating a vast glass and steel canopy that would shelter and unify the Queen Elizabeth Hall, the Purcell Room and the Hayward Gallery under one roof, along with many of the terraces and walkways around them, enabling the creation of fresh amenities. Although the proposals attracted interest and attention, they were later abandoned by the Southbank Centre.

PETER SHEPHEARD (1913–2002)
Architect, landscape architect, artist and author Peter Shepheard studied at the Liverpool School of Architecture and assisted his godfather, Patrick Abercrombie, with his *Greater London Plan* for the LCC. He designed both houses and housing for the LCC, but was equally respected for his landscape design work, including work on the landscaping of the South Bank Exhibition and London Zoo. Shepheard also wrote a number of influential books on gardens and garden design.

SADIE SPEIGHT (1906–1992)
Architect, designer and author Sadie Speight designed the colourful textile curtains towards the rear of the boxes within the auditorium at the Royal Festival Hall. A founder member of the Design Research Unit, alongside Misha Black, she was married to architect Leslie Martin.

BASIL SPENCE (1907–1976)
The Scottish architect Basil Spence studied at the Edinburgh College of Art and began his career in Edwin Lutyens' office. Early projects embraced Arts & Crafts and Art Deco influences but during the post-war period Spence embraced modernism and, at times, veered into brutalism. For the Festival of Britain, Spence was invited to design the Sea & Ships pavilion, as well as the interiors of the nearby Skylark café. Around the same time, the architect won the competition to design Coventry Cathedral, completed in 1962 and widely regarded as his masterpiece.

STANTON WILLIAMS
Founded by architects Alan Stanton and Paul Williams in 1985, Stanton Williams has worked on many major cultural centres and campus projects, among other projects, including the Central Saint Martins College of Art & Design at King's Cross, London (2011). During the mid-Nineties, the practice was commissioned to work

on a number of updates and amendments to the National Theatre, some of which proved controversial with the theatre's original architect, Denys Lasdun.

RALPH TUBBS (1912–1996)
Architect and writer Ralph Tubbs studied at the Architectural Association before working with the pioneering modernist architect Ernö Goldfinger. This was followed by a period spent assisting Maxwell Fry, covering the latter's partnership with former Bauhaus director Walter Gropius during his brief sojourn spent living and working in Britain. During World War II, Tubbs designed factories producing goods for the war effort and was then appointed to serve as a Festival of Britain architectural design co-ordinator under Hugh Casson. Tubbs was also the architect of one of the most famous temporary pavilions on the South Bank Festival site, namely the Dome of Discovery. With a diameter of 111m (365ft), this futuristic superdome was – apart from the Festival Hall – one of the largest Festival of Britain structures. The Festival also provided the catalyst for the launch of the architect's own practice, with Tubbs' later projects including the Granada TV Centre & Studios in Manchester (1956/62).

JACK WHITTLE (1920–2013)
Architect Jack Whittle served as the LCC's deputy architect under Hubert Bennett. As such, he was a key part of the team responsible for the evolution of the South Bank during the Sixties, including the design and delivery of the Hayward Gallery and Queen Elizabeth Hall, while Whittle's talents as a violinist helped to inform the acoustic design of the latter as well as the Purcell Room. Later, Whittle was an influential figure at the LCC and its successor, the GLC, particularly in the development of the new neighbourhood of Thamesmead. Eventually Whittle moved on and, in 1971, became Cheshire's county architect.

LEFT The undercroft beneath the Queen Elizabeth Hall and Purcell Room has been adopted as a skate park, as well as becoming a place for other forms of self-expression.

BIBLIOGRAPHY

Colin Amery (ed.), *The National Theatre: An Architectural Review Guide*, Architectural Press, London, 1977.

Mary Banham & Bevis Hillier (eds), *A Tonic to the Nation: The Festival of Britain 1951*, Thames & Hudson, London, 1976.

Christopher Breward & Ghislaine Wood (eds), *British Design from 1948: Innovation in the Modern Age*, V&A Publishing, London, 2012.

Nicholas Bullock, *Building the Post-War World: Modern Architecture and Reconstruction in Britain*, Routledge, London, 2002.

Barnabas Calder, *Raw Concrete*, William Heinemann, London, 2016.

Carmody Groarke, *BFI Southbank*, Carmody Groarke, London, 2022.

Peter Carolin & Trevor Dannatt (eds), *Architect, Education & Research – The Work of Leslie Martin: Papers & Selected Articles*, Academy Editions, London, 1996.

Susannah Charlton & Elain Harwood (eds), *100 Buildings 100 Years*, Batsford, London, 2019.

Becky E. Conekin, *'The Autobiography of a Nation': The 1951 Festival of Britain*, Manchester University Press, Manchester, 2003.

Peter Cook (ed.) *Archigram*, Princeton Architectural Press, New York, 1999.

Ian Cox, *The South Bank Exhibition*, H.M. Stationery Office, London, 1951.

W.J.R. Curtis, *Denys Lasdun: Architecture, City, Landscape*, Phaidon, London, 1994.

Trevor Dannatt, *Modern Architecture in Britain*, Batsford, London, 1959.

Robert Elwall, *Building a Better Tomorrow*, Wiley-Academy, Chichester, 2000.

Allen Eyles et al, *NFT50: A Celebration of Fifty Years of the National Film Theatre*, BFI, London, 2002.

GLC, *GLC Architecture 1965/70*, Greater London Council, London, 1970.

Miles Glendinning, *Modern Architect: The Life & Times of Robert Matthew*, RIBA Publishing, London, 2008.

Christoph Grafe, *People's Palaces: Architecture, Culture & Democracy in Post-War Western Europe*, Architectura & Natura, Amsterdam, 2014.

John Grindrod, *Concretopia*, Old Street Publishing, Brecon, 2013.

Elain Harwood & Alan Powers (eds), *Festival of Britain*, Twentieth Century Architecture 5, Journal of the Twentieth Century Society, London, 2001.

Elain Harwood, *Space, Hope and Brutalism: English Architecture 1945–1975*, Yale University Press in Association with Historic England, New Haven & London, 2015.

Elain Harwood & James O. Davies, *England's Post-War Listed Buildings*, Batsford/ Historic England, London, 2015.

Elain Harwood, *Brutalist Britain: Buildings of the 1960s & 1970s*, Batsford, London, 2022.

Owen Hopkins, *The Brutalists: Brutalism's Best Architects*, Phaidon, London, 2023.

Jude Kelly et al, *Respecting Brutalism: The Hayward Gallery & Queen Elizabeth Hall at 50*, Feilden Clegg Bradley Studios, London, 2018.

Ian Latham (ed.), *Allies & Morrison*, Right Angle Publishing, London, 2011.

Philip Long & Jane Thomas (eds), *Basil Spence Architect*, National Galleries of Scotland, Edinburgh, 2007.

John McKean, *Royal Festival Hall*, Phaidon, London, 2001.

Charlotte Mullins, *A Festival on the River*, Penguin, London, 2007.

Geoffrey Nowell-Smith & Christophe Dupin (eds), *The British Film Institute, the Government & Film Culture, 1933–2000*, Manchester University Press, Manchester, 2012.

Simon Phipps, *Brutal London*, September Publishing, London, 2016.

Kenneth Powell, *Powell & Moya*, RIBA Publishing, London, 2009.

Alan Powers, *Modern: The Modern Movement in Britain*, Merrell, London, 2005.

J.M. Richards, *An Introduction to Modern Architecture*, Pelican, London, 1970.

Daniel Rosenthal, *The National Theatre Story*, Oberon Books, London, 2013.

Jean Symons, *Royal Festival Hall: Concert Hall Notebook*, Architectural Association, London, 2000.

Barry Turner, *Beacon for Change: How the 1951 Festival of Britain Shaped the Modern Age*, Aurum, London, 2011.

Christine Wall et al, *The Art of Concrete: Building the South Bank Arts Centre*, University of Westminster, London, 2012.

INDEX

ACKNOWLEDGEMENTS

The authors would like to express their sincere thanks to the staff of the Southbank Centre, the National Theatre, the British Film Institute and the London Eye for their valued assistance in the research and production of this book, with particular thanks due to: Sarah Bemand, Anoushka Chakrapani, Miles Clemson, Camilla Dervan, Laura Gosney, Chloe Heywood, Osita Olisa, Liz Parkinson, Richard Pickard, Gabi Thomas, Rachel Tomlin, Jasper Watkins, Susannah Browning and Clare Wood. We would also like to express our gratitude to the following: Luke Engleback, Feilden Clegg Bradley, Lauren Hawkins at Carmody Groarke, Dawn Hepburn at Haworth Topkins, Tina Persaud, Steve Tompkins at Haworth Tompkins, Simon Willmoth and the staff of the RIBA Library as well as Polly Powell, Nicola Newman, Bella Skertchly, Eoghan O'Brien and all the team at B.T. Batsford. Photographer Rachael Smith would also like to thank the following for their assistance during the photographic shoots for this book: Anna Chip, Fiona De Lys, Marcia Morgan and Henry Rowbotham.

ABOUT THE AUTHOR

Dominic Bradbury is a journalist and lecturer specialising in architecture and design. He has written for *Wallpaper*, *World of Interiors*, *Elle Decoration*, *Vogue Living*, the *Telegraph* and the *Financial Times*. His books include *The Atlas of Mid-Century Modern Houses*, *Mid-Century Modern Complete*, *New Brazilian House*, *The Iconic House*, *The Iconic Interior*, *Mountain Modern* and *Waterside Modern*. He lives in Norfolk.

ABOUT THE PHOTOGRAPHER

Rachael Smith is one of the leading architectural and interiors photographers in the UK. Her work has featured in *World of Interiors* magazine for many years and she also contributes to a wide variety of other leading publications, including *The Guardian*, *The Observer*, *The Times*, *Elle Decoration* and *House & Garden*, as well as numerous magazines abroad. Smith's recent books include *Victorian Modern*, *London Shop Fronts* and *Dungeness: Coastal Architecture*, and she is currently working on a number of new book projects. She lives in Stamford.

First published in the United Kingdom
in 2024 by
Batsford
43 Great Ormond Street
London
WC1N 3HZ

An imprint of B. T. Batsford Holdings Limited

ISBN 978 1 84994 807 4

A CIP catalogue record for this book is available from the British Library.

10 9 8 7 6 5 4 3 2 1

Reproduction by Rival Colour Ltd, UK
Printed and bound by Toppan Leefung Printing International, China

This book can be ordered direct from the publisher at www.batsfordbooks.com, or try your local bookshop.

FSC
www.fsc.org
MIX
Paper | Supporting responsible forestry
FSC® C104723